Phonology:

A Cognitive View

Tutorial Essays in Cognitive Science

Advisory Editors

Donald A. Norman
Andrew Ortony

Phonology:

A Cognitive View

Jonathan Kaye
University of London

LEA LAWRENCE ERLBAUM ASSOCIATES, PUBLISHERS
1989   Hillsdale, New Jersey   Hove and London

Lawrence Erlbaum Associates, Inc., Publishers
365 Broadway
Hillsdale, New Jersey 07642

Library of Congress Cataloging-in-Publication Data
Kaye, Jonathan, 1942–
    Phonology : a cognitive view / Jonathan Kaye.
        p.   cm.
    Bibliography: p.
    Includes index.
    ISBN 0-89859-858-3.   ISBN 0-8058-0466-8 (pbk.)
    1. Grammar, Comparative and general—Phonology.
2. Psycholinguistics. I. Title.
P217.K34 1988   88-24695
414—dc19   CIP

Printed in the United States of America
10 9 8 7 6 5 4

To my mother

Contents

Preface

This book is designed to acquaint the reader with the field of phonology: the study of the systems of linguistically significant sounds. No previous exposure to the field of linguistics is assumed and indeed this book is not directed toward an audience of professional linguists. I begin with a brief introduction to the field of linguistics and to the place of phonology within this field as well as its principal problems and objectives. The question of the nature of phonological units will be taken up here. This is a theme that recurs throughout this book as we proceed through the various phases of the evolution of linguistic theory.

In the following chapter I present the kinds of phenomena that are of interest to phonologists. The study of these phenomena leads to a series of hypotheses concerning the form of phonological representations and the units of which they are composed. The principles of classical generative phonology are introduced here. This approach, developed a little less than 20 years ago by Noam Chomsky and Morris Halle, has had a profound impact on modern phonology. The phonological rule, the formal basis of the description of phonological processes in this framework, is introduced.

The next chapter contains some speculation concerning the existence of phonological phenomena. I offer some arguments against phonetically motivated phonological processes. The status of the "standard theory" is evaluated. I show that this theory provided a truly novel way of viewing phonological systems. On the other hand, problems internal to this theory have led to major revisions and striking new directions of research. These new directions are taken up here. The reader is presented highlights of phonological research undertaken in the wake of classical generative phonology.

Chapter 4 follows the evolution of non-linear phonological representations. The theoretical innovations first presented in chapter 3 are extended to other domains. The notion of phonological tiers is developed. The reader is presented the skeleton, the central core of phonological representations.

The final chapter is devoted to current issues in phonological theory and some speculation as to the directions it may take in the years to come. I discuss the implications of recent findings for such fields as automatic speech recognition, phonological parsing, and machine learning.

This book is in no way intended as an exhaustive and objective view of the history of and current practices in phonology. The views expressed, although shared to a greater or lesser extent by some of my colleagues, are by no means the unanimous (and perhaps not the majority) opinion of today's phonologists. Of course, ideas differ as to "nuts and bolts" questions of particular formal mechanisms that one wishes to insert into a phonological theory. More importantly, there are fundamental divisions concerning what phonology is and why it is worth investigating the phenomena that make up its subject matter. I make every effort to indicate clearly the controversial aspects of my discussion. It is inevitable that certain points may escape such treatment. The reader desirous of obtaining other points of view is therefore urged to consult the available literature on phonological theory.

Discussion of the various issues raised in this book requires the citation of examples from a variety of different languages. I try to minimize the burden to the reader by limiting the use of exotic symbols. I employ the following conventions for presenting phonological data:

1. Words cited in the standard spelling of their language will be enclosed in quotes, with the parts to which I wish to draw attention, italicized (e.g., "see", "oiseau").
2. Translations of foreign language examples will be enclosed in single quotes (e.g., "manger" 'to eat').
3. Phonetic forms will be enclosed in square brackets (e.g., "seek" [si:k]).
4. Phonological forms will be italicized (e.g., wazo "oiseau" 'bird').

This book has a markedly cognitive orientation. In recent years linguists have been influenced to an ever greater extent by research in various branches of such fields as cognitive psychology and computer science (learning theory, artificial intelligence). This influence has been reciprocal with linguistic results assuming a greater interest for practitioners of the above mentioned disciplines. Within linguistics itself, evidence supporting a given theoretical position is no longer limited to internal data of the sort provided by linguistic analyses of a given system. Issues such as parsing, "learnability," child language acquisition, and aphasia form a significant part of the grist for the linguist's mill. Such issues are raised throughout this work and should make clear what I mean by a "cognitive orientation."

Having read this book, the reader should (if I have done my job well) have a reasonable idea of what phonological theory is about, what the questions are that it is designed to answer, and why anybody should care. Phonology is an area of linguistics that has held my interest for over 20 years. Aside from all the normal, sound, scientific reasons for being involved in this field, and in spite of the fact that it can be maddeningly frustrating, I do phonology because it is basically a lot of fun. If I can portray phonology in such a way that one can understand (if not share) this point of view, then writing this book will have been worth the effort.

My sincere thanks go to my friends and colleagues who have had the kindness to make me believe that I have something worth saying. What merit this work may have is largely due to their influence. The manuscript benefited greatly from their comments and suggestions. I alone should be blamed for any shortcomings.

A final word of thanks must be added to the two editors of this series: Donald Norman and Andrew Ortony. They deserve much of the credit for rendering this work accessible to non-linguists, catching my numerous errors of style and spelling, eliminating what could be eliminated and asking for clarifications where such were needed. I am extremely grateful to them for their tireless efforts.

1

Introduction

WHAT IS LINGUISTICS?

Phonology may be defined as the study of the systems of linguistically significant sounds. At this point such a definition is rather meaningless. First, we need to know what "linguistically significant" means. When does a sound have this property? How do we know? Clearly "linguistically significant" must mean something like "of significance to linguists or to the object of their study." It is reasonable then to begin our discussion of phonology with an explanation of the nature and the goals of linguistics. A clear idea of the field will provide us with a setting in which we can properly place phonology.

I should make it clear at the outset that the portrait of linguistics that I am about to sketch is by no means the only one. The field of linguistics represents a variety of different scholarly traditions, and each one carries its conception of what it is about (see the volume by Morgan, in prep., in this series). Linguistics departments may be found in the faculties of humanities, social sciences, behavioral sciences, and natural sciences. Such diversity is not purely administrative. People called linguists have dramatically different views as to what it is they are studying, what kind of results they are looking for, and how such results should be interpreted. I emphasize again that I will not present a balanced, objective, and comprehensive view of linguistic theory and practice nor of that branch of the field that deals with problems of a phonological sort. The conception of linguistics that I am

1

about to present may be characterized rather broadly as that of *generative grammar*. This approach, proposed in its initial form by Noam Chomsky in the mid 1950s, has certainly become the dominant school of linguistic theory both in terms of the numbers and the geographic diversity of those who utilize it. As is to be expected, the field of generative grammar has constantly evolved in the course of the last three decades.[1] It would be inaccurate to characterize it today as a single approach. It represents rather a family of approaches sharing a certain vision of the field but differing in fundamental ways in both form and content.

What is it then that linguists study? A standard joke among linguists is that the first question one gets asked after having revealed one's profession is "Oh, so you're a linguist. How many languages do you speak?" The general view is that a linguist is somebody who studies languages and consequently winds up speaking a lot of them. It is true that some linguists speak an impressive number of languages, but this is typically due to personal taste and opportunity rather than to professional necessity. It is quite untrue, however, that linguists study languages. Indeed, it is unclear what it would mean to study languages (beyond learning to speak, read, or write them).

In fact, what linguists study is not languages but rather the particular systems that underlie them: linguistic systems or grammars. What then is a system that underlies language? In a word, linguists do not study languages but rather *Language* or, more precisely, that cognitive faculty that underlies our linguistic capabilities. Why should anyone believe that such a thing exists? To answer these questions we must consider what it means to "speak a language." Following Chomsky, we can assume that this implies the ability to produce and to understand an unlimited number of sentences proper to the language in question and that the overwhelming majority of these sentences have never been heard or uttered before. In our day-to-day world, most of what we hear and speak is novel. A moment's reflection suffices to convince oneself that these novel utterances pose no particular difficulty. We produce and understand them with no apparent effort.

This is all well and good, but what does it tell us about the linguistic systems that underlie this ability? We have seen that speaking a language implies the ability to produce and understand a potentially infinite class of utterances or sentences. Furthermore, for any particular individual, this ability is limited to a tiny subset of the world's languages. The ability to speak, say, English does not have as an automatic consequence the ability to speak Zulu, French, or Navajo. This means that speakers of English possess a particular knowledge that permits them to speak and understand this language. Those who do not speak English do not possess this particular

---

[1]The volatile nature of generative grammar has displeased a number of scholars who apparently prefer a more static approach. Hagège (1976) is a good example of this thinking.

knowledge. They will possess a knowledge of whatever language or languages they happen to speak. We call this knowledge *linguistic competence*. It must be borne in mind that I am employing the term *knowledge* in a very special way, that is, I do not mean *conscious* knowledge. Speakers of English are no more able to express the nature of this knowledge than they are to explain the stereoscopic nature of their vision or the manner in which they recognize people they know. It is the understanding of the exact nature of this linguistic competence that is the primary objective of linguistics.

This characterization of linguistic competence can aid us in determining certain properties of the linguistic systems that are its source. For example, it is quite clear that our linguistic system cannot be simply a list of sentences. Such an hypothesis encounters serious difficulties: In the first place, there are an unlimited number of sentences associated with any human language. The storage capacity of the human brain, while doubtless quite large, is nevertheless finite. Second, it is difficult to imagine a scenario for acquiring a linguistic system that is a list of sentences. I have already pointed out that the vast majority of linguistic utterances are novel; they have never been heard or produced before by the individual in question. This excludes simple imitation as a learning theory. One cannot imitate something one has never heard before.

There are a number of ways (some trivial) in which we can illustrate the unlimited nature of linguistic competence. Consider the sentence:

(1) I ate 42 oranges.

Clearly, one can replace the integer in (1) by any other and the result will still be a grammatical English sentence. In coordinate constructions (those involving *and, or,* etc.), there is no obvious limit on how many terms may be conjoined. For example:

(2) I ate an apple and a pear, and a peach, and an aardvark, ...

Expressions such as noun phrases (a noun possibly accompanied by various articles, modifiers, quantifiers, and so on) may themselves contain noun phrases. This recursivity once more leads to a potentially infinite number of utterances, as in (3).

(3) I ate the apple that the boy whom Harry saw yesterday threw at the fence that the girl painted with the brush that fell from the truck that John's brother drove . . . .

Sentence (3), while stylistically somewhat strained, is perfectly comprehensible. Notice that there is no point at which it must be terminated. It may be extended indefinitely in the ways already mentioned.

The three examples also illustrate the fact that we cannot consider a language to be a list of words. A list of words, being a list, runs into the same sort of difficulties that we have just discussed vis-à-vis sentences. There are other problems. Anyone who has attempted to understand a newspaper written in a foreign language using only a dictionary has a small idea of what these problems are. Let us consider some very simple examples.

(4) John saw Jane.

Sentence (4) consists not only of three words but of certain grammatical relations that connect them. Any speaker of English knows that in (4) *John* is the agent, that is, the one who sees, and *Jane* is the object or patient, the one who was seen. Changing the order of these words changes or destroys the meaning. Thus, (5a) does not mean the same thing as (4), and (5b) and (5c) are not possible English sentences.

(5) a. Jane saw John.
     b. *Saw Jane John.[2]
     c. *John Jane saw.

Thus, in addition to knowing English vocabulary, a speaker must know the principles of sentence construction: the syntax. To a certain extent, these principles may vary from language to language. If we simply translated (4) word for word into Japanese or Desano (a South American Indian language) the resulting form would be quite ungrammatical. In fact, (5c) would be the corresponding form in both these languages. In a similar vein, in English a verb such as *look* requires a preposition, whereas a verb such as *discuss* does not.

(6) a. Mary looked at the pictures.
     b. *Mary looked the pictures.
     c. Mary discussed the equation.
     d. *Mary discussed of the equation.

In French, the facts are exactly the reverse. The verb *regarder* (look at) must not be followed by a preposition, whereas the verb *discuter* (discuss) requires one.

(7) a. Marie a regardé la fille. ('Mary looked at the girl'.)
     b. *Marie a regardé à la fille.

---

[2]Ungrammatical sentences are, by convention, preceded by an asterisk.

    c. Marie a discuté de l'équation. ('Mary discussed the equation'.)
    d. *Marie a discuté l'équation.

As a final example, question words such as *who, what, when, where,* and so on, typically appear at the beginning of sentences in many languages. English and French behave in this way.

(8) a. John ate *an apple.*
      What did John eat?

    b. Jean a mangé *une pomme.*
      Qu'est-ce que Jean a mangé?

In a number of other languages these question words appear in the same position as their nonquestioned counterparts. In Jula, a Mandé language of the Ivory Coast, direct objects precede the verb. If the direct object position is questioned (*What did John eat?*), the question word appears in exactly this position and not at the beginning of the sentence as in English and French.

(9) Mùsó   yé   *màrò* dúmú ('The woman ate rice'.)
    woman past rice eat

    Mùsó   yé   *mù*   dúmú ('What did the woman eat?')
    woman past what eat

    Mù mùsó yé   dúmú
    what woman past eat

    We see that to a certain degree linguistic systems may differ from one language to another. The question then arises as to just how different two linguistic systems may be. Put another way, to what extent do grammars of different languages share the same properties? A rather extreme view—to the effect that grammars could vary in arbitrarily many ways—was expressed by certain linguists during the 1940s and 1950s (e.g., Joos, 1958, p. 96). Resemblances that were found among various linguistic systems were treated for all practical purposes as accidents. Notions such as *linguistic relativism,*[3] borrowed mainly from anthropology, flourished during this

---

[3]Whorf (1956) is a prime example of this view. Linguistic relativism, simply put, is the view that the form of the grammar of a language influences the world view of the speaker of that language. More or less implicit in this view is the belief that each language should be studied in its own terms. What may be true of, say, English should not be automatically applied to any other language.

period. Today, this view is generally rejected by linguists. Results of linguistic research on an ever-growing number of different languages indicates clearly that grammatical systems are largely identical, with variation occurring in well-defined areas and the degree of variation being quite restricted. In the final example of linguistic variation discussed previously, it was noted that some languages may place question words (*who, what,* etc.) at the beginning of a sentence or they may remain in situ, that is, direct objects in direct object position, subjects, in subject position, and so on. This seems to exhaust the possibilities. No language appears to place question words at the end of a sentence, at least not systematically. No language has them after the third word, in the middle, and so forth. Question words are either left in place or they are fronted to the beginning of a sentence. That's it!

The claim that languages (read linguistic systems) are pretty much the same may seem controversial. Obviously, languages are different enough to prevent us from understanding every one of them. The differences seem impressive when one leafs through various grammar books of different languages. This feeling is natural enough given the fact that informal observations involving different languages or even dialects (varieties of the same language) stress differences and not similarities. However, it turns out that the bulk of what constitutes a grammar is common to all human languages. Pedagogical grammars invariably emphasize linguistic differences, therefore it is not surprising that only the tip of the grammatical iceberg is dealt with in these works.

A few examples drawn from the linguistic literature (principally from Chomsky) will illustrate the kinds of phenomena that are found in all linguistic systems.[4] Consider first the following sentence:

(10) *John* said that *he* was sick

Sentence (10) is ambiguous. The pronoun *he* may either refer back to John (John himself is sick) or to some other individual (John said that he [i.e., Bill] was sick). In contrast, (11) does not display the same ambiguity.

(11) *He* said that *John* is sick.

In (11), *he* cannot refer to *John;* rather, it must refer to some individual other than John. Oversimplifying somewhat, we could say that if a pronoun

---

[4]The ensemble of syntactic, morphological, and phonological properties that are presumed to be common to all linguistic systems have been termed *universal grammar* (UG). Under one interpretation, UG is posited as making up part of the human biological endowment. Aspects of UG are innate and not learned. Readers wishing to know more about the syntactic issues discussed here are invited to consult Morgan (in prep.).

refers to some other noun in a sentence, it must be preceded by that noun.[5] This is not a fact peculiar to English. Indeed, it is difficult to imagine how such a phenomenon could be learned. It is rather a general property of the relationship between a pronoun and its antecedent. Similar sentences in an impressive variety of languages display identical properties.

(12) *French*
Jean a dit qu'*il* est malade. (ambiguous)
Il a dit que *Jean* est malade. (unambiguous)

Dutch
Jan heeft gesegd dat *hey* ziek is. (ambiguous)
Hey heeft gesegd dat *Jan* ziek is. (unambiguous)

Berber (Morocco)
Abdal i-nna   is   *i*-fulki.   ('Abdal said that he is handsome' ambiguous)
Abdal he-said that he-handsome

I-nna   is   *Abdal* i-fulki.   ('He said that Abdal is handsome' unambiguous)
he-said that Abdal he-handsome

Hausa (Nigeria, Niger)
Mùsá   yá cèè *yáá* gàjí. ('Moussa said he is tired' ambiguous)
Moussa-he said   he tired

Yáá céé *Mùsá*   yá gàjí. ('He said Moussa is tired' unambiguous)
He   said Moussa-he tired

Wolof (Senegal)
Muusa   wax-na ne   def-*a* feebar. ('Moussa siad that he is sick' ambiguous)
Moussa said-he that is-he sick

Wax-na ne   *Muusa*   def-a feebar. ('He said that Moussa is sick' unambiguous)
said-he that Moussa is-he sick

It seems reasonable to suppose that properties concerning the relationship between pronouns and their antecedents are not part of the grammar of a particular language but rather belong to the common core of linguistic properties shared by all human languages: what we can call universal grammar. Similarly, languages permit questioning of a number of

---

[5]This is indeed an oversimplification. A pronoun may refer to a following noun in sentences such as:

(i) After *he* washed the dishes, *John* took a nap.

Sentence (i) is not at all problematic for the claim that we are considering here, but a complete analysis of this phenomenon would carry us too far afield.

grammatical positions such as subject, direct object, and indirect object. For example, starting with a sentence such as:

(13) *The boy* (subj.) gave *a book* (d. obj.) *to Mary* (ind. obj.).

one can question the subject:

(14) *Who* gave a book to Mary?

the direct object:

(15) *What* did John give to Mary?

and the indirect object:

(16) *To whom* did John give the book?
(or informal English, *Who* did John give the book to?)

Again, this is not a fact peculiar to English. The same could be said for any other language. In contrast, there are grammatical positions that cannot be questioned. There is no way to question grammatical positions embedded within a relative clause.

(17) John saw the boy who gave *a book* to *Mary*.

In (17) one cannot question the position represented by *a book* or by *Mary*. Attempts to do so result in such monstrosities as:

(18) a. *What did John see the boy who gave to Mary?
b. *To whom did John see the boy who gave the book?

If these sentences are horrible, it is not because they are meaningless. There are perfectly reasonable interpretations that could be associated with both (18a) and (18b). These are given in (19a) and (19b).

(19) a. John saw the boy who gave something to Mary; what was that thing?
b. John saw the boy who gave a book to someone; who did he give a book to?

The ungrammaticality of the sentences of (18) is due to some principle of grammar. Indeed, sentences corresponding to those of (18) are ungrammatical in all known human languages. The fact that these sentences are ill formed is not a property of English but rather reflects some underlying principle of universal grammar.

To sum up, we have seen that linguistics is concerned with the grammatical systems that underlie human languages. A primary task of linguistics is to separate those aspects of grammar that are common to all linguistic systems from those that are peculiar to a particular language or set of languages. In addition, linguistics attempts to characterize the manner and extent of grammatical variation, that is, how grammars of different languages may vary from one another. Grammatical subjects exist in all languages. In some, they precede the verb; in others, they follow the verb. There is no language, however, where, for example, a subject precedes the verb in sentences with an odd number of words and follows it in sentences with an even number of words. There is no language where subjects are found in the middle of a sentence. Such formal properties (*middle of, odd, even*) are easy to express and to understand. Nevertheless, they are not present in human grammars.

Related in obvious ways to the questions already considered is that of the projection problem: How can a child acquire a language based on the scanty and nonsystematic sample to which he or she is first exposed? Clearly, the child has a head start. This head start consists of a biologically programmed capacity to acquire and utilize a linguistic system. This capacity is related in obvious ways to what we have called universal grammar. To the extent that there exists a common core of grammar, the burden of acquisition is correspondingly reduced. Universal grammar can be viewed as being hard wired into the child. The task of acquisition is then simply to fix the particular aspects of the linguistic system to which the child is exposed: Do *wh*-questions words move to the beginnings of sentences or not? Do direct objects precede or follow the verb? And so on. Acquisition becomes, in effect, the selection of language-specific features from among a limited set of possibilities. It should be clear then that results of linguistics concerning the nature and scope of universal grammar and the range of linguistic diversity will have a direct impact on hypotheses concerning language acquisition.

WHAT IS PHONOLOGY?

We have seen that linguistics deals with the various systems that constitute a grammar. What are these systems? The examples given in the previous section dealt mainly with the way sentences are organized. The subsystem of grammar dealing with principles of sentence construction is called *syntax*.

One can also study the organization and composition of words, which is called *morphology*. Morphology deals with a variety of subjects, such as the formal processes of word formation. Words may be formed by other words by means of *suffixation: happy–happiness, prefixation: do–redo,* and so forth. These various morphological processes have effects that are of interest. In the first example, appending the suffix -*ness* changes a grammatical category (*happy* is an adjective, *happiness* is a noun), whereas no such change occurs in the second case (both *do* and *redo* are verbs). Some morphological processes affect the argument structure (the relationship between a syntactic head and its arguments) of a word. For example, the verb *last* is intransitive as in *The game lasted four hours.* Adding the prefix *out-* creates the transitive verb *outlast* as in *Mary outlasted Bill.*

The branch of linguistics called *semantics* deals primarily with questions of meaning and logical form. Sentences like

(20) Mary wants to marry a man with red hair.

are ambiguous with respect to what is called the scope of the verb *want.* Sentence (20) can mean either that there is a man with red hair and Mary wants to marry him or that Mary is interested in marrying any male with red hair. The problem of scope is but one of a variety of subjects that are dealt with in semantics.

This leaves phonology (along with phonetics, which is dealt with in a later chapter) as the remaining branch of linguistics. As I noted at the beginning of this chapter, phonology deals with systems of linguistically significant sounds. What can be said about such systems and why they are worth worrying about? Let us begin by trying to imagine what possible content a field such as phonology could have. It is hardly a revelation that words, the constituents of sentences, are not unanalyzable atoms but rather are themselves composed of units. Many of the world's writing systems reflect this internal structure. In writing systems, words are composed of letters and it is these letters that generally correspond to the word-internal units.[6] Let us designate that set of all these units as &*alphabet.* Studying the nature of &alphabet will furnish a better understanding of what phonology is about.[7]

---

[6]Two qualifications must be made here: (a) Not all writing systems have symbols corresponding to these word-internal units. The Chinese system uses ideograms, one of which may represent a word or a major constituent of a word. Other systems are syllabic, that is, each symbol represents a syllable rather than an individual sound. Japanese *kana,* and to some extent the Hebrew and Arabic writing systems, are syllabic in nature. (b) In systems such as English, one character does not always represent a single sound, and one sound is not always represented by a single character. The symbol *x* often represents a sequence of two sounds, namely [ks]. The sequence of symbols *th* represents the initial unitary sounds of *thin* [θ] and *then* [ð].

[7]To begin this discussion, the term &*alphabet* refers to a set of letters or graphemes that are related to the written language. In later sections I use the set &alphabet to refer to a set of

Let us start with the simplifying assumption that &alphabet is a set of characters representing individual sounds found in the languages of the world. For the time being, let's assume that &alphabet is the set of 26 lowercase letters.[8] Having established this fact, it would appear that there is nothing more of interest to say about a phonological system. Indeed, if we consider artificial languages such as computer languages, our description is largely true. Basically, one needs to know only the set &alphabet(X), where X is the language in question. Once the membership of &alphabet is established, there appears to be little more to say on the subject. Certain sequences of these characters may have a reserved meaning in the language in question: *RUN, PRINT, LOAD, SAVE* are some commands in the language BASIC. There are, however, no constraints as to what sequences of &alphabet(BASIC) could constitute a command. The command *LPRINT* ⟨*text*⟩ causes text to be sent to the printer. The fact that the initial sequence of characters *LPR* is unpronounceable in English is of no importance in BASIC or, for that matter, in any other programming language. The notion of illicit sequence of characters is foreign to programming languages.[9] On the other hand, many programming languages impose length restrictions on various units. Thus, many varieties of BASIC limit variable names to single characters for numbers and single characters followed by $ for strings. Such length restrictions are totally foreign to natural languages. There is no human language that requires nouns to have, say, three units.

In sum, programming languages require (a) that the set &alphabet be defined, perhaps as a list of reserved symbols, (b) a definition of a well-formed term (e.g., a variable may not begin with an integer), and that's pretty much all. This is hardly engrossing material let alone the stuff on which to base a branch of linguistics. If serious individuals under no coercion spend entire careers studying phonology, there must be more to it than what has been said with respect to programming languages. We have already seen some indications of fundamental differences between the two systems: human and machine. Human languages make no use of size restrictions on their constituent units. Machine languages have no constraints

---

sounds (or, more precisely, a set of symbols representing those sounds). The reader should be aware of this dual utilization (letter/sound). The context of the discussion will dictate which interpretation to give to &alphabet (letter or sound?)

[8]It should be clear that this assumption is completely false. If we imposed the requirement that each sound unit is represented by exactly one character, the inventory of human sound units would require far more than 26 characters.

[9]This statement must be qualified somewhat. Certain languages prohibit integers at the beginning of variable names. A character such as the back slash (\) often has a special meaning and cannot be freely used in strings. If one limits oneself to the 52 upper- and lowercase characters, the absence of restrictions on sequences is a property of almost all programming languages.

of the sort, *LPR* is an ill-formed sequence. In a later chapter I explore the reasons for these differences.

Let us look a bit more closely at the possible nature of &alphabet for the class of natural languages. In this discussion, &alphabet refers to a set of sounds rather than a set of letters. A reasonable question is whether &alphabet is identical for every language. In other words, are the units that compose words always the same? The answer is no. Comparing even such closely related languages as English and French (as opposed to, say, English and Japanese, which do not belong to the same linguistic family) suffices to demonstrate that &alphabet(English) $\neq$ &alphabet(French). Concretely, French has a series of front rounded vowels,[10] found in words such as *cru* 'raw', *bleu* 'blue', and *heure* 'hour', that do not exist in English. Similarly, English as two interdental fricatives,[11] found in words such as *thin* and *rather,* which do not exist in French. The same demonstration could be performed for practically any two languages, with the same results. Furthermore, the example demonstrates that &alphabet(English) &alphabet(French) are not in a subset relation. In fact, the majority of the units involved are common to both languages but there are, as we have seen, units of French that do not occur in English and vice versa.

Keeping in mind that &alphabet is referring to a set of sounds, phonology could be characterized as the specification of &alphabet(X), where X is some language. We could then define &alphabet as the universal pool of units from which each linguistic system draws some subset. This view of phonology is riddled with difficulties. We have defined the phonological inventory (the list of sound units) of a language X as &alphabet(X): some subset of &alphabet. This is tantamount to claiming that any subset of &alphabet is a potential phonological inventory. One could imagine writing down the symbol for each sound unit on a piece of paper, putting them all into a hat, and drawing out some number of them. The chances of constituting a phonological inventory that in any way resembles a human system is quite remote. First, there is the question of size. A human phonological inventory will usually consist of between 20 and 40 sound units. Second, not just any collection of these units will do. Certain units are nearly always present in phonological inventories. Others are relatively rare. The presence of a sound unit X may imply the presence of a sound unit Y. That is, inventories may be found with Y alone or with X and Y but never with X and not Y. One of the major tasks of phonology is to define the set &alphabet (i.e., the set of possible human speech sounds) as well as

---

[10]Front rounded vowels are pronounced with the tongue toward the front of the oral cavity, as in English *beat, bet,* but accompanied by lip rounding.

[11]Interdental fricatives are sounds characterized by noise (friction) produced by the tongue being placed between the teeth.

&alphabet(X) for some arbitrary X (i.e., possible phonological inventory) and to formulate hypotheses to account for the implicational relationships that hold between different segments. This by no means exhausts the problems to which phonologists address themselves. To carry this discussion further requires some reflection on the nature of what I have been calling phonological units. This is the subject of the following section.

PHONOLOGICAL UNITS

Let us now consider the units that constitute the set &alphabet. These are the building blocks from which words are constructed. Their existence is hardly surprising from an engineering point of view. People typically know sets of words whose numbers run into the tens of thousands. Suppose, contrary to fact, that a word were represented by an unanalyzable block of something. A system requirement would then be the ability to produce and recognize thousands of these blocks in a reasonable time span, often under conditions that are less than ideal (noisy environment, distractions, communication at a distance, etc.). Given such a system, the demands made on the human production and recognition system would be considerable. The problem of accessing these unanalyzable blocks (words) would be far from trivial. Developing a reasonable scenario to account for the fact that humans can understand with relatively little difficulty different dialects of their own language, not to mention the production of nonnative speakers (foreign accents), is a complex feat. If words were unanalyzable blocks, it would be difficult to explain why speakers, say from Texas, who pronounce the words *pen* and *pin* alike, cause no particular problem for speakers who do not. That two words, which are distinct in some dialects, may become homophones in other dialects is not problematic. All languages contain homophones (e.g., English *sea* and *see*). The claim is that speakers will make adjustments for such mergers without having to learn the new pronunciations *as new words*. One notices that a word like *pin* is pronounced differently, but one does not learn this form as a new lexical item. In contrast, a North American English speaker must learn the British English word *lift* as equivalent to *elevator*. These two processes are quite different, yet treating words as blocks would render this distinction impossible. Indeed, the fact that it is these two words, *pen* and *pin,* that merge rather than, say, *pin* and *Carthagenian* would have to be treated as an accident. Be that as it may, it is clear that words are *not* unanalyzable blocks. They are composed of units. Let us now consider these units in some detail.

We have defined &alphabet to be the set of all possible sound units available to linguistic systems for the composition of words. The set &alphabet(X) represents the inventory of sound units for a language X. We have already seen that words are not unanalyzable blocks but are composed of these units. We can now raise the same question with respect to the units themselves: Are they unanalyzable blocks or do they also have an internal organization? Put another way, can these sound units be classed into sub-groups that have some linguistic significance? If so, what is the basis of this classification? It is instructive to compare these units to those utilized by a microcomputer. To pursue this example, let us consider a phonetic alphabet consisting of 26 characters. Each character is to represent some speech sound. Limiting ourselves to the set of lowercase letters {a, b, c, . . . , z}, we note that each letter is typically represented by a seven-digit binary number as in (21):[12]

(21)	Bit Number	7	6	5	4	3	2	1
Letter								
a		1	1	0	0	0	0	1
b		1	1	0	0	0	1	0
c		1	1	0	0	0	1	1
d		1	1	0	0	1	0	0
e		1	1	0	0	1	0	1
f		1	1	0	0	1	1	0
g		1	1	0	0	1	1	1
h		1	1	0	1	0	0	0
i		1	1	0	1	0	0	1
j		1	1	0	1	0	1	0
k		1	1	0	1	0	1	1
l		1	1	0	1	1	0	0
m		1	1	0	1	1	0	1
n		1	1	0	1	1	1	0
o		1	1	0	1	1	1	1
p		1	1	1	0	0	0	0
q		1	1	1	0	0	0	1
r		1	1	1	0	0	1	0
s		1	1	1	0	0	1	1
t		1	1	1	0	1	0	0
u		1	1	1	0	1	0	1
v		1	1	1	0	1	1	0
w		1	1	1	0	1	1	1
x		1	1	1	1	0	0	0
y		1	1	1	1	0	0	1
z		1	1	1	1	0	1	0

[12]Example (21) gives what are called the ASCII (American Standard Code for Information Interchange) values for the characters in question.

Such a binary representation offers a multitude of possible classes, none of which are particularly interesting from a linguistic point of view. These units may be organized in an ascending order (as shown), which represents the alphabetical order of our writing system but which has nothing to do with any phonetic or phonological properties of the sounds that these symbols represent. It should be clear that this order (i.e., our traditional alphabetical order) is completely arbitrary. It has no underlying linguistic significance. Other types of subgrouping produce similar results. If we take the class of units whose third bit is equal to 1, we obtain the set {d, e, f, g, l, m, n, o, t, u, v, w}: a set of no conceivable significance. Similar exercises utilizing this internal organization of units are equally futile.

In sum, the machine-internal representation of sound units of the sort shown in (21) is perfectly arbitrary. One may recover the collating sequence, which is associated with the writing system of a language like English, but this is completely external to the question of the mental representation of sound units in human languages. English would remain English if it were written using another collating sequence, say, {q, w, e, r, t, . . . b, m, n}; another alphabet, say, Arabic; or even if it had no associated writing system at all. The question remains: Are the internal representations of human sound units as arbitrary as the internal machine representations of our familiar alphanumeric character set? In other words, are the internal representations of sound units worth studying? The answer to this question emerges from the study of phonological phenomena that are the subject of the next chapter.

2

Phonological Phenomena

THE NATURE OF PHONOLOGICAL
PHENOMENA

The most remarkable fact about phonological phenomena is that they exist at all. In the previous chapter we looked at the main branches of linguistics: syntax, morphology, semantics, and phonology. One can easily find analogues to syntax and semantics in artificial languages such as programming languages. With a bit more effort one can even find phenomena reminiscent of morphology (words with internal composition). The programming language *C* allows $++$ and $--$ as prefixes and suffixes that may be appended to variables. If *count* is a numeric variable of a given value, executing $++$ *count* will cause the value of count to be increased by one. Similarly $--count$ will cause the value of count to be decreased by one each time it is called. Phonological properties of programming languages are a bit harder to come by. One obvious reason is that these and other artificial languages are not spoken. I return to this factor later in this chapter.

Forgetting for the moment the nonspoken nature of programming languages, let us try to imagine what phonological phenomena would be like in such systems. A programming language will have an alphabet from which its various commands, variable and constant names, data, and so forth, will be drawn. Thus, in BASIC a command such as *PRINT* consists of five characters, *P, R, I, N,* and *T,* drawn from &alphabet(BASIC). The form of the command *PRINT* does not vary from one statement to another, as the following examples show[1]:

(1) PRINT A$ 'Print out the value of the string variable A$'
     PRINT Q$ 'Print out the value of the string variable Q$'
     PRINT X   'Print out the value of the numeric variable X'
     PRINT "Hello world"   'Print out *Hello world*'

It would be astonishing if one were to come across a version of BASIC in which the statements in (1) were written as in (2).

(2) PRINA A$
     PRINQ Q$
     PRINX X
     PRIN" "Hello world"

In the examples of (2), this exotic dialect of BASIC has four different forms for the same command, call it *PRINT*, PRINA, PRINQ, PRINX,* and *PRIN"! What's more, additional forms for PRINT* appear if we add more examples.

(3) PRINM M
     PRIN5 5231
     PRINF F$

Continuing the investigation of this mythical BASIC, one finds that one cannot freely use the various forms of the PRINT* command in any context. For example, the statements of (4) invariably elicit the response *Syntax error,* which is BASIC's somewhat misleading way of saying that it does not recognize the initial word of these statements as a command.

(4) PRIN" A$
     PRINA Q$
     PRINQ X
     PRINQ"Hello world"

Furthermore, a given form of the PRINT* command reappears in other statements.

---

[1]In BASIC, the command *PRINT* has a synonym *?*. I am not referring to this kind of variation here.

(5) PRINX X$
PRINX X CHR$(27)
PRINX X "is the number of psychologists who adore Vivaldi"

The form of the *PRINT** command in this invented BASIC is not constant. It varies as a function of what follows. Informally, one can express the form of the *PRINT** command as follows:

(6) The PRINT* command consists of five characters. The first four are constant, namely, *PRIN*. The fifth character of the command is variable, being a copy of the first character of the following argument.

It is difficult to imagine why anyone would think of formulating a command having this form. It is not surprising that context-dependent variables such as the *x* in *PRINx* in our mythical BASIC dialect are completely absent from real programming languages. The situation that I have just described is nevertheless absolutely typical of human languages. The context-dependent variable is but one example of a phonological phenomenon, the subject of this chapter, and there is no human linguistic system that does not manifest such phenomena.

Let us consider a very simple phonological phenomenon taken from English. The English definite article has a constant written form: *the*. It resembles in this way the command *PRINT* in real BASIC.

(7)   *the* boy   *the* girl   *the* house   *the* living room
       the apple   *the* igloo   *the* entrance   *the* umbrella

Pronouncing these two rows of forms produces an interesting result: The definite article is produced with a final vowel *uh*, which one also finds in words such as *sofa*. The articles of the second row all end in a vowel *ee*, similar to that of *happy*.[2] I am avoiding a technical discussion of the exact phonetic nature of these vowels. What is important, is the fact that the pronunciation of *the* is not uniform but varies according to the context in which it occurs. For ease of exposition let me introduce two phonetic symbols to replace the informal representations *uh* and *ee*. The final vowel of the definite article in an expression such as *the book* is represented as [ə]. The final vowel of the article as pronounced in *the apple* is represented as [i].

---

[2]Notice that *the* can always be pronounced with a final *ee* regardless of the context in cases were one wishes to emphasize some unique aspect of the noun in question: She's THE geophysicist for the job!

The square brackets are used to indicate that the enclosed expression is a phonetic representation. I can now distinguish the two forms of the English definite article by writing th[ə] and th[i].

The observant reader will have noticed that *the* is pronounced th[ə] when the following word begins with a consonant, and th[i] when it begins with a vowel. This phonological phenomenon, the alternation of th[ə] and th[i], may seem trivial and uninteresting but in fact it provides valuable clues concerning the way a phonological system, and ultimately the human mind, is organized. I return to this example later in the discussion. Right now I would like to present another phonological phenomenon much more reminiscent of the *PRINx* command from the mythical BASIC discussed previously. This example is taken from modern Arabic and again involves the pronunciation of the definite article. Let us consider the following forms:

(8) ad dars   'the lesson'   as sayyaaara 'the car'
     ar ruzz   'the rice'   al luɣa   'the language'
     az zubda 'the butter'   an naas   'the people'
     at turb   'the land'   ash shams   'the sun'

In each form of (8) the definite article precedes the noun. It is immediately apparent that the form of the definite article is not invariable but changes according to the initial consonant of the following noun. Using the same formalism employed to describe our *PRINx* command, we can represent the Arabic definite article as aX, where X is a variable whose value depends on the following consonant (i.e., d before d, r before r, etc). The initial a reflects the invariable portion of the form. In other words, the definite article in Arabic begins with the unit a. The following unit is a copy of the initial consonant of the following word.

In fact, the situation is even more interesting. The second unit of the Arabic definite article is not always a copy of the following consonant. In many cases it is a constant like a, the first unit of the Arabic definite article, as the following forms show:[3]

(9) al bab   'the father'   al baab   'the door'
     al firaash 'the bed'   al qamar   'the moon'
     al ɣurfa   'the bedroom'   al kitaab 'the book'
     al miftaaḥ 'the key'   al yasaar 'the left'

---

[3]The reader will note certain unfamiliar symbols in the Arabic examples. These symbols represent certain consonants (not present in English whose phonetic values do not concern us here. They are included for completeness One can treat them as funny-sounding consonants.

Let's sum up the situation of the Arabic definite article:

1. Before a certain subset of &alphabet(Arabic), the form of the definite article is *aX*. Let's call this subset *CorC* for reasons that become clear later.
2. Before words beginning with a member of the complement subset *&alphabet(Arabic)–CorC,* the form of the article is *al*.

This example, taken together with the previous one involving the English definite article (*th*[ə] vs. *th*[i]), is quite revealing as to the structure of phonological units and the nature of phonological phenomena. It is thus useful to explore the nature of phonological segments at this point. We return to our discussion of phonological phenomena afterwards.

THE NATURE OF PHONOLOGICAL SEGMENTS

Let us consider first the structure of phonological segments. In the previous chapter we raised the question of the internal structure of sound units. Are sound units (phonological segments) the ultimate constituents of linguistic structure? Are they atomic, unanalyzable kernels? If they have an internal structure, how is it organized? The first examples of phonological phenomena discussed earlier have a direct bearing on these questions.

The Atomic Hypothesis

Suppose we begin with the hypothesis that phonological units are atomic, that is, unanalyzable. We have seen that each phonological phenomenon involves a bifurcation of the set &alphabet(X), where *X* refers to the language in question. So, in English, the form of the definite article *th*[i] appears before words beginning with a certain class of units, call them *vowels*. The alternative form *th*[ə] occurs before members of the complement set, which we may refer to as *consonants*. All English units belong to one or another of these sets, and none belongs to them both. The definite article phenomenon in English bifurcates the set &alphabet(English) into two subsets: *vowels* and *consonants*. Now the atomic hypothesis (units are unanalyzable) taken seriously must treat this bifurcation as an accident. There is no reason to favor one particular division of the set &alphabet over another. Specifically, one could not appeal to the fact that the subset *vowels* may be characterized by the common property of resonance, because appeal to such a property would go counter to the idea of unanalyzability of segments. I have cheated a little in using terms like *consonants* and *vowels,* whose very definitions run counter to the atomic hypothesis—they make reference to the internal properties of sound units. Let us pretend for the moment that these names are as arbitrary as, say, *subset1* and *subset2*. So far, there is no insurmountable problem for the atomic hypothesis. The bifurcation dictated by the English definite article is quite different from that of the Arabic example and this is exactly what one would expect. Notice that the existence of phonological phenomena would remain a total mystery (why have two different forms for the English definite article and a dozen or so for the Arabic definite article?), but let's deal with one problem at a time.

The size of &alphabet(X) varies from one linguistic system (language) to another, with the majority of cases consisting of between 25 and 40 members. If we assume that a phonological inventory consisting of 33 members is fairly typical, we can now calculate the number of possible bifurcations of such a system. The formula is quite simple: $2^n - 1$, where n equals the number of segments in the inventory.[4] This gives us roughly 8.6 billion potential bifurcations for an average phonological inventory. Now, if the game is not rigged and the units are really unanalyzable atoms, the chances of finding the same bifurcation with respect to a different phonological phenomenon are roughly 1 in 8.6 billion. Consider now the English indefinite article *a*. Once again, we find two variants for this form: *a* and *an,* as shown in (10).

(10) a boy   a girl   a house   a living room
      an apple   an igloo   an entrance   an umbrella

We see at once that the distribution of *a* and *an* is exactly parallel to that of *th*[ə] and *th*[i]. The former occurs before the subset we have called consonants and the latter before vowels. The chances of this happening (i.e., finding the same bifurcation in two independent phenomena) is 1 in 8.6 billion. It seems that we are pretty lucky.

Now, one might pose two objections to this argument. First, both examples come from the same language, English. Second, both examples involve the same grammatical category: the article. The first argument makes sense if one wishes to claim that the choice of a bifurcation is made once (or at least a reasonably small number of times) and that this bifurcation is applied to the various phonological phenomena of the language in question. If such were the case, this would eliminate much of the force of the two English examples. In fact, the claim is false, but more of this later. The tacit assumption behind the second argument is that similar grammatical categories will involve similar bifurcations. A rapid comparison of

---

[4]We subtract one to eliminate the empty set. This would correspond to phenomena that occur in no environment. We include the subset including all members of the set to allow for context-free phenomena.

the English and Arabic cases, both of which involve the definite article, shows this to be untrue.

The weakness of these objections notwithstanding, let us take another example from English that does not run afoul of either of them. This example involves a phenomenon of a different sort: a variation in pronunciation among different English dialects. This sort of dialectal variation is also grist for the phonologist's mill. It is the sort of thing one would like to understand. Let's take two English dialects. For convenience I'll call one *New York* and the other *London,* although the phenomenon that I describe is by no means restricted to these two cities. Nor is it the case that every speaker from each city pronounces the words in question in the manner presented. Nevertheless, the phenomenon exists and is generally, if not universally, true for the populations in question. What is involved is the pronunciation of the segment [y] (as in *yoyo, yacht, yeast,* etc.) following certain consonants. In a word like *pure,* for example, you will notice that the segment *y* immediately follows the initial segment *p.* I will use a quasi-phonetic notation to indicate the pronunciation: [py]ure. In both New York and London, this word is pronounced with the initial sequence *py.* There are, however, words which are not pronounced in the same way in the two dialects. For example, *tune* is pronounced in New York with an initial *t* but with no following *y,* [t]une. In London, the same word is pronounced [ty]une. So, there are some words that are pronounced the same way, at least at the beginning, and others that are pronounced differently. The puzzle is how to characterize each group. Can we predict if a word will be pronounced the same or not with respect to this phenomenon? The following examples are organized in two groups. The first is pronounced the same in both London and New York; the second is pronounced differently in the two locales.

(11) a.

New York	London	Word
[py]ure	[py]ure	pure
[by]ureau	[by]ureau	bureau
[ky]ute	[ky]ute	cute
ambi[gy]uity	ambi[gy]uity	ambiguity
[fy]ew	[fy]ew	few
[vy]iew	[vy]iew	view
[my]usic	[my]usic	music

b.

[t]une	[ty]une	tune
[d]ew	[dy]ew	dew/due
[s]ue	[sy]ue	sue
re[z]ume	re[zy]ume	resume
[n]ew	[ny]ew	new

The examples in (11) illustrate another bifurcation of the set &alpha-bet(English). This bifurcation, of course, is only relevant for the New York dialect. In (11a) we see the consonants after which the [y] is pronounced; in (11b) we have a sample of the consonants after which the [y] is not pronounced. Neither (11a) nor (11b) is exhaustive but they may be assumed to be representative of the behavior being discussed here. Let us consider the forms of the left column of (11b). These are the consonants after which [y] is not pronounced in the New York dialect. The consonants involved are: *t*, *d*, *s*, *z*, and *n*. Here is the remarkable thing: All of these consonants exist in Arabic and all of them belong to the subset CorC. Recall that this is the set of consonants before which the Arabic definite article displayed its variant forms. The relevant examples are found in (8) and (9). The consonants that behave exactly alike in the New York and London dialects with respect to the retention of [y] are (among others): *p, b, k, g, f, v,* and *m*. In each case, if the consonant exists in Arabic, it is a member of the complement set &alphabet(Arabic)–CorC. Abstracting from differences in the sets &alphabet (Arabic) and &alphabet(English), we find two bifurcations that are virtually identical. If sound units are really unanalyzable atoms, it is hard to explain why such parallelism should occur.

I should emphasize here that this situation is absolutely typical of the vast majority of phonological phenomena. Analyzing a new phonological system inevitably brings about a feeling of déjà vu. Similar phenomena may vary somewhat from one system to another, but this is generally due to other factors that are also at work. It is not indicative of any fundamental differences among the phenomena themselves. Let's compare English and Japanese. In informal spoken English, many speakers pronounce sequences involving our friend [y] in a special way. I list these sequences with their resulting (informal) pronunciation as follows:

(12) *t* + *y* = *ch*   I know wha*t y*ou want = wha[ch]ou
      d + *y* = *j*   Did *y*ou . . . = Di[j]ou
      s + *y* = *sh*   kis*s y*our . . . = ki[sh]our
      z + *y* = *zh*   has *y*our . . . = ha[zh]our

This process is by no means obligatory. Speakers may choose to pronounce *t* + y as *ch* or as *t* + *y*, but the pronunciations in (12) do commonly occur, and they are what interest us here.

In Polish, not a language normally regarded as being very similar to English, the virtually identical phenomenon occurs. The context is somewhat different: In Polish, we find instances of phenomena like those in (12) within words rather than between two words. Furthermore, the sequences *d* + *y* and *t* + *y* result in *j* and *ch* only when they follow another consonant.

The following examples illustrate this phenomenon in Polish:[5]

(13) *t* + *y*   post + yā   'they fast'   [posčow̄]
     d + *y*   jezd + yā   'they travel'   [yezj̈ow̄]
     s + *y*   kos   + yā   'they mow'   [košow̄]
     z + *y*   mroz + yā   'they freeze'   [mrožow̄]

Furthermore, such cross-linguistic similarities can be found with respect to a great number of other phonological phenomena. The slogan of phonological analysis would appear to be "(Almost) nothing new under the sun." Restricting ourselves to the bifurcation issue and the question of phonological representation, we sense that something is clearly amiss in the atomic unit hypothesis. If phonological units are viewed as nothing more than different colored marbles, then why do they repeatedly manifest the property of grouping themselves into classes? Why do the same classes keep occurring in language after language? Under the circumstances, the most prudent approach is to abandon this atomic notion of phonological units. We are led to the conclusion that phonological segments have internal structure. In the following sections, we investigate the form and the substance of this structure.

The Phonetic Classification of Phonological Units

It has been common knowledge for centuries that phonological units do not group themselves randomly, but rather form classes that recur both in the same language and across language boundaries. The examples of the previous section gave some indication of this fact. Many of the groupings seem so natural that they are taken entirely for granted. Recall the behavior of the English definite and indefinite articles. One set of forms (*th*[i], *an*) appears before words beginning with the subset of segments we called vowels. A second set (*th*[ə], *a*) occurs before consonants. These terms have entered the common parlance and so it is easy to forget their status with respect to the processes just described. In fact, they behave in ways quite similar to the subset CorC, which we discussed with respect to the Arabic definite article and the behavior of [y] in New York English. Of course, consonant, vowel, and CorC do not exhaust the classes of segments that can be derived from the study of phonological phenomena. They are but a small part of a very large story. In order to follow the line of reasoning that leads to the phonologist's view of the internal representation of segments, we need not

---

[5][č] is the phonetic symbol used to represent the *ch* sound. [š] is used for *sh* and [d], for *j*.

consider other cases for the moment. The reader should bear in mind, however, that the examples given earlier are absolutely typical of the situation found in other phenomena and in other languages.

Thus, it seems that certain groups of segments behave as classes with respect to phonological phenomena. What does this tell us about their internal structure? There is always the possibility that it tells us virtually nothing! We have demonstrated by an informal statistical approach that segments must be assumed to have internal properties. There is no logical necessity that these properties have a direct mapping onto other aspects of the real world. These classes of segments defined by these properties could be completely arbitrary; they could have no defining attributes besides their membership in the classes themselves. This is to say that one could propose that there is no logical necessity that the class vowel or CorC or any other that we might uncover in the course of a phonological analysis consist of the specific segments we have discussed. We could imagine another world with other sorts of humans where a class that we called vowels consisted of the segments *p, i, r, x,* and *o.* Is there any reason to believe that our world is somehow more natural than this latter one? The reader should recall that these phonological classes must be assumed to be part of the innate cognitive system of our species. The same classes recur in all the languages of the world. This is not to say that every language exploits every class in some obvious fashion. What is meant here is that if we constructed a universal set of classes derived from the phonological phenomena of all languages, each language would exploit a substantial subset of this universal set and any class derived in one language would be found in many others. Furthermore, it should be borne in mind that phonological phenomena are not the only manifestation of nor evidence for the segmental classes that we are now investigating. Be that as it may, we cannot consider that the classes found in English are in any way peculiar to that language. If these classes are arbitrary and accidental and have no defining features, this is not a property of one particular language; it is a property of our biologically defined linguistic capacity.

In fact, it is quite obvious that these classes are anything but random. From its beginnings, a major part of the content of phonological theory has been devoted to the question of the defining features for these classes. It was assumed early on that each phonological segment is a composite of a series of properties or features. Phonological classes are then the set of all segments who share a particular property or properties. The properties that characterize these classes were assumed to be *phonetically* based—that is, segments are grouped according to the way they are pronounced.

Consider the class CorC that was discussed with respect to Arabic and New York English. Based on the examples in (8) and (11b), this class contains the following segments: *t, d, s, z, r, l, n, sh*.[6] What property do these segments have in common? Try pronouncing a *p* as in the nonsense syllable *puh*. Notice that the lips are pulled together, completely closing off the oral cavity (the mouth). Pressure is built up in the oral cavity behind the lips and eventually the closure is released. Because the pressure within the mouth is greater than the atmospheric pressure outside the mouth, the air rushes from the oral cavity in the direction of the lesser pressure, causing an audible sound: the sound of *p*. Consider now the pronunciation of *t* as in *tuh*, a member of the subset CorC. Notice that the pronunciation of *t* does not involve closing the lips. Rather, the tip of the tongue is raised, placing it in contact with the area just behind the upper teeth and sealing off the remainder of the oral cavity. The rest of the story is similar to that of *p*; pressure builds up behind the closure and the contact is released allowing the air to pass out of the mouth. Now try to pronounce in turn *duh, suh, zuh, ruh, luh, nuh*, and *shuh*. You should notice that in each case the tip or the blade of the tongue (the area of the tongue just behind the tip) is raised and placed in contact at or near the back of the upper teeth. This is the phonetic characterization of the class CorC. Segments possessing this phonetic property are called *coronals*. This explains the use of the term CorC for the Arabic and English classes. It stands for Coronal Consonant.

This is a truly remarkable correlation—one of the foundations of all of phonology:

1. The class of consonants in Arabic in front of which the final consonant of the definite article is variable can be characterized as all and only those consonants whose pronunciation involves raising the tongue tip or blade toward the top of the mouth.

2. The class of consonants in New York English after which a [y] is not pronounced (in contrast with London English) are all and only those consonants whose pronunciation involves raising the tongue tip or blade toward the top of the mouth.

Thus, classes of segments that exhibit similar behavior may be defined in phonetic (articulatory) terms.

This result is far from trivial. It is quite conceivable that no such correlation exists. Indeed, this was the initial hypothesis of this section. That phonologically defined classes—that is, classes based on phonological behavior such as the examples given—may be defined phonetically gives us an enormous insight into the manner in which segments are organized and

---

[6]The subset CorC is incomplete both for Arabic and for English. This does not affect the force of the argument. Although written with two letters in English orthography, *sh* represents a single sound.

constructed. At the same time, it is only by virtue of the existence of phonological considerations that linguistic phonetics, the study of the articulatory and acoustic properties relevant to human speech, is possible.[7] Even the notion of a phonological segment itself is nontrivial and far from evident in the absence of phonological data (and hence a phonological theory), as anyone working on the segmentation problem in the field of automatic speech recognition has quickly learned. There is no simple algorithm for reading off segments from a spectrogram, from x-ray movies of the vocal tract, or from any other representation of the speech signal or the articulatory gesture that accompanies it. In this sense, the segmentation problem is similar to certain aspects in vision research. Edge detection goes well beyond a trivial mapping of the series of intensity readings supplied by the neural cells in the retina. Notions as fundamental as *edge* require the intervention of higher order cognitive processes, be the edges visual edges or auditory ones. In the absence of phonological evidence, it would be impossible to know which of the myriad of conceivable organizational criteria is relevant for human speech perception and production.

So far, we have seen that at least one phonologically defined class is amenable to phonetic characterization: CorC. The classes vowel and consonant are also definable in phonetic terms. For reasons that become clear later, the definition of these classes is by no means as clear cut as that of CorC. As a very rough approximation, we can characterize vowels as those segments whose primary articulatory property involves a resonating cavity. Consonants involve a blockage, either complete or partial, of the airstream. To get a feel for this distinction, one should compare the pronunciation of *p* as in *puh* with that of the vowel *a* pronounced *ah* ("open your mouth and say *ah*"). As we have seen, the former segment involves a complete closure at the lips. In the latter case, the mouth is wide open. The position of the tongue (lowered to the bottom of the oral cavity) gives the appropriate form to the resonating cavity, yielding the characteristic quality of this vowel.

It is not my intention to give here an exhaustive description of the phonetic properties relevant to phonological behavior. The reader may consult introductory texts in phonology and phonetics for a more detailed

---

[7]Too often the importance of this point is missed in discussions of phonetics and phonology. Phonetic variables must be correlated with *something*. Logically, they are not established prior to investigations of phonological systems. To illustrate, imagine studying the articulation of segments if the atomic hypothesis discussed in the preceding section were true. If not infinite, the number of phonetic (articulatory and/or acoustic) criteria that one could utilize to describe segments is extremely large and diverse. One could group sounds according to the total energy involved in their production, according to the number of different muscles involved in their articulation, their length in milliseconds, the distance an articulator moves from some predefined neutral position, and so on.

description. Rather, my aim is to lay out the theory of phonological representations: what its claims are and the evidence on which they are based. Having established that phonetic properties underlie phonological representations, we may now inquire as to their formal properties. For example, are phonetic properties binary (on or off, yes or no) or are they scalar? Morris Halle, the father of modern phonology, suggested over 30 years ago that all phonological features are binary, at least in so far as their phonological behavior is concerned. Applying this question to the class CorC, what we are asking is whether saying a given segment is coronal or not is sufficient to explain phonological behavior involving this property. Could one imagine a system where consonants ranged along a scale of coronality and that this scale was relevant to phonology? Given the definition of a coronal consonant, one whose articulation involves raising the tip or blade of the tongue toward the top of the mouth, the scalar interpretation seems unlikely. Either the tongue is raised or it is not. It is hard to conceive of a middle ground in this case. Many other phonological features are also binary in an obvious way. For example, in some dialects of Texas English, the vowel *i* as in *bit* and *e* as in *bet* are pronounced the same when they appear before certain consonants. The words *bit* and *bet* are indeed distinct in these dialects, but *pin* and *pen, him* and *hem* are pronounced identically. The merger of these two vowels takes place before the consonants *m* and *n* and nowhere else. What do these consonants have in common phonetically? They are known as nasal consonants. They are characterized by the articulatory gesture of lowering the velum, the soft part of the roof of the mouth immediately behind the palate. Lowering the velum opens the nasal passage and permits the air to escape through the nose. Nasalization is therefore another property of phonological segments. Again, it is difficult to imagine this feature as scalar. Either air passes through the nose or it doesn't.

One could imagine a scalar classification of consonants ranging from the front of the mouth, say for a *p,* to the back of the mouth, for a *k.* The consonant *t* and the sound *ch* would represent intermediate positions along this scale. Although such a classification is possible, it is not manifest in observed phonological phenomena. The classification derived from phonological events always seems to call for binary rather than scalar values of some property. Halle's conjecture of the 1950s appears to have stood the test of time.[8] Given the binary nature of phonological features, it is natural to represent them with the values + and −. Segments that are members of the

---

[8]The binary hypothesis is generally but not universally accepted by phonologists. Lass (1984) has recently argued for the existence of scalar features. I do not find his arguments convincing. I will continue the discussion of phonological representations assuming that all phonological properties are binary.

class CorC are designated [+coronal]; all other segments are designated [−coronal].

A second question involves the number of properties defining a bifurcation stemming from a phonological process. The class CorC obtained from Arabic and English involved only one feature—coronal. Are bifurcations, then, always limited to just one property? To answer this question, let us consider another phonological phenomenon. This time the data are from Quebec French.[9]

(14)	Quebec French	European French	Translation
	t^{s}ype	type	type (n)
	t^{s}u	tu	you
	tout	tout	all
	thé	thé	tea
	taux	taux	rate
	pâteux	pâteux	doughy
	tas	tas	pile
	d^{z}ire	dire	to say
	d^{z}ur	dur	hard
	doux	doux	soft
	dé	dé	dice
	dos	dos	back
	deux	deux	two
	date	date	date

In these examples, we see the consonants *t* and *d* appearing before a variety of different vowels. In European French, the two consonants are invariably pronounced *t* and *d*. In Quebec French, they are pronounced as in European French except before two vowels: *i* and *ü*.[10] Before these vowels, *t* is pronounced *t^s* (a sound similar to *zz* as in *pizza*) and *d* is pronounced *d^z* (similar to *ds* as in *lads*).

What sets these vowels apart from all other vowels of French? Let us first consider the position of the tongue on these two vowels. Compare the pronunciation of the sound *ee* with that of *ah*. Say one sound after the other and notice what your tongue is doing. It should be clear that the tongue is held in a much higher position for *ee* than for *ah*. This is why the doctor says, "Open your mouth and say *ah*" and not, "Open your mouth and say

---

[9]I will use conventional French spelling except where the phenomenon in question manifests itself.

[10]This vowel is written *u* in French orthography. It does not exist in English. It is a vowel similar to *ee* as in *seek* but with rounding of the lips as is done for the vowel *oo* as in *boot*.

ee." Pronouncing a vowel that involves raising the body of the tongue would not provide the doctor with a clear view of your throat. The French vowel *ü* involves the same tongue position as the French vowel *i* (similar to English *ee*). The former vowel is pronounced with rounded lips, but the latter is not. We can say, then, that the French vowels *i* and *ü* possess the property of having the tongue body in a high position. We can represent this property as [+high].

Thus far, this example looks similar to the ones involving the class CorC (= [+coronal]). It appears that all we need to say is that in Quebec French, *t* is pronounced *t^s* and *d* is pronounced *d^z* before [+high] vowels. There is one hitch however: *i* and *ü* are not the only French vowels that are [+high]. Try pronouncing the sounds *oo* (as in *boot*) and *ah*. You should notice the same effect that was previously observed for *ee* and *ah*. The tongue is clearly raised for the vowel *oo*. We have already seen that the vowel *ah* does not have this property. The French vowel *u* (spelled *ou*) is [+high]; yet *t* and *d* are pronounced as in European French (cf. *tout* and *doux*). It is therefore insufficient to characterize the class of vowels before which *t* and *d* undergo modification as [+high].

To sum up, *i* and *ü* trigger this process but *u* does not. All three vowels are [+high]. What do *i* and *ü* have in common that *u* does not? Repeatedly pronouncing the pair of vowels *ee* and *oo* should give us an indication of the difference. You should notice that after pronouncing the vowel *ee*, the tongue slides toward the back of the mouth to produce an *oo*. Suppose we classify *oo* as [+back] and *ee* as [−back]. French *ü* will also be [−back]. Recall that there is no difference in tongue position between *i ü*. We can now characterize the class of vowels that triggers this phenomenon. It is precisely the intersection of the set of vowels that are [+high] and the set of vowels that are [−back]. This intersection has two members in French: *i* and *ü*. In standard phonological notation, the way of representing this intersection is by means of a feature matrix. The feature matrix for the class that interests us here is given as follows:

(15) $\begin{bmatrix} +\text{high} \\ -\text{back} \end{bmatrix}$

Both feature specifications are necessary if we wish to define the class of vowels containing only *i* and *ü*. Failure to mention the specification [−back] gives us the vowels *i* and *ü*, which we want, but also the vowel *u*, which we don't. The feature specification [+high] is also necessary. The class of vowels that are [−back] includes once again *i* and *ü*, but it also contains *e* (similar to English *ay*, as in *day*). It will be recalled that *e* does not trigger the process under study here, that is, in Quebec French one says *thé* and not *t^s hé*.

We see then that classes derived from phonological phenomena may involve more than one feature.

Let us continue to use this Quebec French example a bit longer. In all the examples that we have considered to this point, phonological classes have defined the sets of segments that *trigger* phonological processes. We also may define phonological classes as sets of segments that *undergo* phonological processes—and their definition may require more than one phonological property as well. Let us consider the class of segments that undergo the Quebec French process. This set has two members: *t* and *d*. The reader will recall that both these consonants belong to the class [+coronal], which we saw earlier. However, [+coronal] also includes several other consonants in French, namely *s, z, r, l, n,* and so on. Of this set only *t* and *d* undergo the process. No other coronal consonant is involved. Our phonological representation in terms of feature matrices gives us the means to define this class of segments. We first need to ask the question: What distinguishes *t* and *d* from other coronal consonants? The pronunciation of these two consonants involves the complete closure of the vocal tract. As long as the articulation is maintained, no air escapes from the mouth or nose. Such sounds are commonly referred to as *stops*. If we add stop as another phonological property of segments, the class of sounds that undergoes the Quebec French process can be defined by the following matrix:

(16) $\begin{bmatrix} +\text{coronal} \\ +\text{stop} \end{bmatrix}$

The number of phonological properties (or features) can be extended such that we are eventually able to define individual speech sounds in terms of these matrices. With enough features we can define any segment in any language. The total number of such features may run from 20 to 30. This gives us the possibility of defining from 2^{20} to 2^{30} different segments.[11] Thus, features play a dual role: They are the ultimate constituents of phonological segments, and they are the medium for the expression of phonological processes. This conclusion should not be too surprising. While it is true that phonological segments are cognitive (i.e., a product of mind) rather than strictly physical (i.e., articulatory or acoustic), there must be some relationship between the cognitive structures that are phonological

---

[11]This assumes that feature specifications are independent of one another; that the value of one feature has no effect on the value of another. In fact, certain feature values imply certain others. Thus, the number of postulated human speech sounds does not reach these theoretical limits. Even with this proviso, feature systems allow for an impressive number of segments.

representations and the physical cues to which they are tied. For example, parsing requires a physical signal as input. It is reasonable to assume that this signal will be translated into a cognitive structure by a process that is, at least in part, driven by this signal. Phonological features, or other segment constituents, must be linked, however indirectly, to some aspect of the physical signal. In like manner, cognitive representations must be mapped onto a set of instructions to the articulatory system. Muscles or muscle groups must be activated to produce oral speech. Put another way, the phonetic interpretation of these cognitive structures may be irrelevant for the internal functioning of the phonology, but it is surely vital when peripheral systems (auditory, articulatory) are involved. That is, it is required for considerations of I/O, (i.e., input/output).

We have seen that the classes of segments that trigger and that undergo phonological processes may be defined in terms of feature matrices. In the standard generative phonology of the 1960s and early 1970s, phonological processes were indeed described using these representations. In this approach, the formal mechanism for the expression of a phonological process is a *phonological rule*. The phonological rule must tell us three things: (a) the set of segments that undergo the rule, (b) the set of segments that trigger the rule (along with the location of this set with respect to the first set), and (c) the change to the input segments brought about by the rule.

We have already discussed the first two sets. To complete the picture we need only add the nature of the changes that make up a phonological rule. Once again, the changes are expressed in terms of phonological features. The structural change brought about by a phonological rule is a feature matrix. A segment undergoing a rule retains all its original feature specifications save those that are explicitly mentioned in the structural change. The form of a rule is summarized in (17).

(17) $A \rightarrow B/C\_\_\_\_D$
      where A, B, C, D represent (possibly null) feature matrices

A is the feature matrix that defines the class of segments that are to undergo the rule. Any segment that is a member of the set A is a candidate for undergoing the rule.[12] The matrix *B* represents the structural change of the rule. A segment satisfying A and occurring in the appropriate context (see the following) will exit the rule, replacing its original values of the features contained in B by those occurring in that matrix. The slash (/) is to be read "in the context." *C* and *D* represent the left and right contexts, respec-

---

[12]I have defined feature matrices as intersections of sets. Technically speaking, then, an individual segment is not a member of the set A but rather a subset (consisting of one member) of the set A. For convenience, I will refer to segments as members rather than as subsets.

tively. The left and right contexts indicate the position of the triggering segments with respect to those which undergo the rule. This formalism allows for triggering elements to occur to the left (C, D is null), to the right (D, C is null), or to the left and right (C_____D) of the segment that is being modified.

To see how this rule functions in a particular case, consider the following simplified example from English. The form of the English plural (and, in fact possessives and third person singular verb forms) has three different pronunciations: *s* as in *cats*, *z* as in *dogs*, and *e*[*z*] as in *kisses*. Let's consider just the first two cases. In order to write a rule of the form (17), we need to know the values of the four feature matrices involved. We'll pretend that this process only applies to *s*. The smallest feature matrix that defines this consonant to the exclusion of all others will serve in the position A. This matrix would be roughly of the following form:

$$(18) \quad \begin{bmatrix} +\text{coronal} \\ -\text{stop} \\ -\text{voice} \\ +\text{strident} \end{bmatrix}$$

We have already discussed the features coronal and stop. Voicing refers to the vibration of the vocal cords during the production of a segment. Some segments have this property [+voice], others do not [−voice]. Try pronouncing *zzzzzz* and then *sssss*. In the first case you should hear (and feel) a distinct buzzing in the region of your Adam's apple. In the second case no buzzing is present. This is the difference between a voiced sound and a voiceless one. Clearly, *s* belongs to the latter set. I will not go into the definition of the feature *strident*. Suffice it to say that this feature distinguishes *s* [+strident] from another voiceless coronal nonstop, θ, which is the symbol for the *th* sound, as in *thin*. θ is [−strident]. The four features suffice to define the single-membered set {s}—the segment which will undergo this rule.[13]

In order to discuss B we need to know what change this rule is carrying out. We assume that *s* is the input segment and that we want to derive *z* in certain contexts. What features of *s* must be changed in order to get a matrix that defines *z*? In fact, *s* and *z* are pronounced almost identically. The only difference is that in one case we get a buzzing (*z*) and in the other we don't

---

[13]This is by no means the correct analysis nor the correct formulation of this process. For heuristic reasons I have taken great liberties in the formulation and description of this phenomenon. At this point in the discussion, nothing hangs on this distortion. The example is only being used to familiarize the reader with the formalism.

(*s*). This buzzing was associated with the feature specification [+voice]. So, to turn an *s* into a *z* all we have to do is change it from [−voice] to [+voice]. This means that B is simply [+voice].

This brings us to the triggering segments. Because *s* is a suffix, its form is conditioned by the segment occurring to its left. This in turn means that the right context D is null. It now remains to discover the defining properties of the triggering set of segments. Phonological theory predicts that they must have something in common. We need to know after what consonants the English plural suffix is pronounced *z*. The answer follows:[14]

(19) | *Vowels* | pie | pie[z] |
Liquids	girl	girl[z]
Nasals	ham	ham[z]
Fricatives	hive	hive[z]
	fife	fife[s]
Stops	bid	bid[z]
	bit	bit[s]

The English plural suffix is pronounced as [z] following all vowels, liquids, nasals, and some fricatives and stops. Let us consider the latter two cases. In (19), [z] follows the consonants *v* and *d,* whereas *s* is produced after *f* and *t.* Comparing the fricatives *f* and *v,* we see that they are produced with the same articulatory gesture: The upper teeth are placed on or near the lower lip. What distinguishes the two is the buzzing effect that is present for *v* and absent for *f.* In our terms, *v* is [+voice] and *f* is [−voice]. Although less obvious, the same is true for *d* versus *t.* The former is [+voice] and the latter is [−voice]. Therefore, we see that *s* becomes [+voice] when it follows a stop or a fricative that is also [+voice]. This seems quite reasonable. The preceding sound has an influence on the following one.

Now what about vowels, liquids, and nasals that also cause the voicing of *s?* Pronouncing these sounds while touching the throat confirms that they are all voiced. In English, all vowels, liquids, and nasals are voiced; some stops and fricatives are also voiced. We are now in a position to state the definition of the class of segments that trigger the voicing effect of our *s:* It is the class of [+voice] segments. Because the triggering class precedes the suffix, this matrix will occupy position C in our rule. Nothing relevant follows the suffix and so position D is null. We can now put all these ingredients together and formulate the rule concerning the plural suffix *s* in English.

---

[14]A liquid is the set of segments containing *r* and *l.* A fricative is a consonant whose articulation involves friction. The vocal tract is narrowed but not completely blocked. Air is forced through this narrow opening producing friction. Some English fricatives are *s, z, f, v.*

(20) $\begin{bmatrix} +\text{coronal} \\ -\text{stop} \\ -\text{voice} \\ +\text{strident} \end{bmatrix} \rightarrow [+\text{voice}] \ / \ [+\text{voice}]\underline{}$

Rule (20) is interpreted as follows: A segment that is a member of the sets [+coronal], [−stop], [−voice], and [+strident] will become voiced [+voice] when it immediately follows any segment that is a member of the set [+voice]. That's all there is to it!

The rule template in (17) is the cornerstone of classical generative phonology. In principle, any phonological phenomenon should be describable in this form. There are a few bells and whistles that are added but they need not concern us here. The central claim is that phonological processes are of the form (17). We now have a much clearer idea of the nature of phonological representations. They consist of a sequence of matrices, where each matrix is the series of properties that define a given segment. Each property has two possible values: + or − (it is present or it is not). Phonological processes are of the form (17). In a context defined in terms of feature matrices, one or more properties of a member of the class of input segments may be modified.

There are a number of empirical consequences associated with this theory. If we adhere strictly to the principle that input classes and triggering classes can only be defined in terms of feature matrices, then certain combinations of segments are excluded from both groups. For example, there exists no feature matrix that includes all and only p and i as its members. There is no set of properties common to these two segments *and only them.* This means that we should never find a process that involves p and i to the exclusion of all other segments. They may be members of a larger set, but no process should effect them exclusively. In like manner, no process should be triggered by p and i alone. Observation of phonological processes in a large sample of languages indicates that, by and large, these sorts of predictions are correct. The great success of generative phonology with respect to its predecessors was that it gave us a formal device for distinguishing classes of sounds that are phonologically significant from those that are not. In the vocabulary of generative phonology, classes of the former type are called *natural classes,* classes definable in terms of a single feature matrix. We should note that any individual segment forms a natural class because any individual segment is definable in terms of a single feature matrix. The central claim of generative phonology may now be restated.

(21) Phonological processes involve only natural classes.

A phonological analysis, in this theory, consists of the inventory of feature matrices that define the phonological inventory (&alphabet) of the language in question, a list of the phonological processes that are operative in the language, and a list of forms (the lexicon) to which the processes apply.

In the preceding discussion I have slipped in a second idea central to the theory of generative phonology. In order for the ensuing discussion to be clear, it will be helpful to introduce some more terminology. The vocabulary of a language is usually thought of as a list of words (the lexicon): *boy, girl, house, sleep, buy,* and so on. Some words, like the five just mentioned, have no internal meaningful structure. They are composed of segments, but the segments in themselves have no meaning. Are words, then, the smallest units that convey meaning? Consider the plural of *boy: boys.* We can see that *boys* has an internal structure and that the components are meaningful. *boys* consists of *boy* plus *s. boy* means what *boy* means and *s* indicates plurality: We are talking about more than one. *boy* can appear all by itself, when it is singular. *s,* the plural suffix, never occurs alone. It is always attached to the end of something else—a singular noun. We need a term to refer to these minimal units of meaning—a class that will include *boy* and *s* but not *boys,* because this latter is not minimal. These minimal units of meaning are called *morphemes.* Morphemes may be *bound* or *free.* Bound morphemes (e.g., *s*) never occur by themselves. Free morphemes may appear as independent words (e.g., boy). The English lexicon contains morphemes that are nouns, verbs, adjectives, and so forth, as well as all kinds of prefixes and suffixes that make up words with internal structure: *-s, re-, -ing, -ed,* and so on. Now, another fundamental claim of generative phonology concerns the form of morphemes. It is stated as:

(22) Each morpheme has a unique lexical representation.

Let us consider first the cases where (22) applies, which is the overwhelming majority of cases. We have already discussed the fact that the English plural morpheme may be pronounced in several ways: [s] and [z], among others. What (22) means is that each of the variant pronunciations of the plural morpheme is derivable starting from a single source: the lexical representation. The discussion of the plural form and the formulation of the voicing rule (20) assumed that the lexical form of this morpheme is *s.* The plural rule says that this morpheme will indeed be pronounced [s] unless it is preceded by a voiced segment. In that case, it is pronounced [z]. Another major part of phonological analysis consists of choosing the input form (the lexical representation) of the various morphemes of the language. The phonological processes are then applied to this input form and the result should be the observed phonetic forms (the output) of the language. The input form is typically a word, with or without internal structure. The input form along with the series of changes (if any) effectuated by the various phonological processes (rules) of the language and the phonetic form (the output) comprise what is known as a *phonological derivation*. We can now see how we arrive at two pronunciations of the English plural suffix starting from a unique source. I give the (simplified) derivations for *dogs* and *cats* in (23).[15]

(23) *Input*   dog + s   cat + s
    Rule (20)   dog + z   not applicable
    Output   dogz   cats

The top line of (23) contains the input forms: the noun followed by the unique form of the plural suffix (*s*). The + is simply an indication of the separation between the noun and the suffix. Rule (20) is now applied to these forms. In the case of *dog* + s, its conditions are satisfied. The suffix *s* matches the input class, and its left context contains a member of the set of voiced segments (*g*). The rule does its work and changes the feature voice from − to + in the matrix of *s*. The result is a matrix that defines *z*. In the case of *cat* + s, rule (20) may not apply. The segment *s* is present and thus part A of the rule is satisfied. However, part C, the left context, is not. For the rule to apply, *s* must be preceded by a segment belonging to the set [+voice]. *t,* the segment preceding *s,* does not belong to this class of sounds, therefore (20) does not apply and no changes to the input form take place. The final line of the derivation gives an informal representation of the pronunciation of these two words. Crucially, *dog* + s is pronounced with a final [z] and *cat* + s, with a final [s]. In real life, derivations are much longer than those of (23). Phonological systems may contain an impressive number of rules. The rules are sometimes ordered with respect to each other. Each rule applies to the output of a preceding rule. The first rule applies, of course, to the input form. Several changes may occur in the course of a derivation.

Earlier, I implied that there are cases where (22) does not apply. Exceptionally different forms of the same morpheme cannot be derived from a single source. These cases are rare. They are usually called *irregular forms* in grammar books. They are difficult to learn and are often eliminated in favor of forms following the regular pattern—forms derivable from a single source. Let me give one example. In English, short adjectives have a comparative form that uses the suffix *-er*.

---

[15]For ease of exposition I use conventional English spelling except for the form of the plural suffix. In a more formal rendition of a derivation we would, of course, be using feature matrices and not symbols (letters).

(24) *Adjective*   *Comparative*

      hot   hotter
      cold   colder
      sad   sadder
      happy   happier
      sick   sicker

However, take the case of *good*. Given the forms in (24), one would expect in a reasonable world that the comparative form of *good* would be *gooder*. Of course, this is untrue. The form is *better*. Notice that we can still recognize the comparative suffix *-er* in this form. But what is the adjective? If we lop off *-er* from *better,* that leaves us with *bet* (or *bett*). Now, we have two phonetic variants for one adjective: *good* and *bet*. There is no way that we can derive one from the other or both from another source. We are stuck with *good* and *bet*. At this point, phonologists (correctly) bite the bullet and put both forms in the lexicon. We, as English speakers, simply have to memorize the fact that the comparative form of *good* is *better* and not *gooder*. This is a violation of principle (22). Such violations exist, as I have said, but they are rare. It is not surprising that children (and some adults) regularize the comparative form and use *gooder* rather than *better*. Be that as it may, principle (22) holds in the overwhelming majority of cases in English and in every other language.

The reader should now have a general idea of the nature and scope of phonological analysis within the theory of classical generative phonology. We have seen how segments are represented and the reasons for these kinds of representations.

Our initial study of phonological phenomena has given some indication of the form that phonological representations may have. If it is assumed that these phenomena are related, directly or indirectly, to some form of cognitive processing, one would like to propose that the representations that appear best suited to deal with such phenomena are an initial hypothesis as to what mental representations are like. As we progress through more sophisticated models of phonology, the representations that emerge may be viewed as more refined hypotheses concerning the nature and structure of phonological representations as they exist in the mind. We shall see that there is growing evidence, both from recent developments in phonological theory and work on phonological processing, that indicates that the phonological feature is not the appropriate unit for these mental representations. This question is raised again in a later chapter.

Finally, we have looked at several phonological phenomena and seen the way such processes are formulated. We have noted that different manifestations of the same morpheme may be derived from a single starting point: the lexical representation of the morpheme in question. I have omitted a number of details, some quite important, but this is a fairly accurate picture of how phonology was done in the past. What is far from clear is why any rational person would want to spend his or her time doing this sort of thing. What does any of this have to do with linguistics as a cognitive system? What possible interest is there in supplying the world with phonological analyses of the sort I have described? Clearly, there has to be something more to phonology. Take heart! There is something more and what that something is the subject of the next chapter.

3

The Search for Explanations

In the previous chapter I gave an overview of the theory of classical generative phonology. The starting point for the description of this theoretical approach was a discussion of phonological phenomena. The processes that modify input strings to phonological derivations are omnipresent. Much of the theoretical work done in phonology has dealt with how best these processes should be formalized. From the beginning, concern with empirical considerations has played a major role in these theoretical discussions. The fact that classical generative phonology provided a formal system capable of distinguishing classes of segments that behaved in a similar fashion with respect to these processes (the natural classes) was considered a definite advantage. Merely describing these processes is of no particular interest. There are, however, a number of questions that one might ask regarding the nature of phonological processes and ultimately the organizational principles of linguistic structure. If, as we assume here, linguistic structure reflects a part of human cognitive capacity, linguistic theory, including phonological theory, holds out the promise of revealing how certain facets of this capacity are organized. It is far from obvious what a list of phonological processes from a variety of languages tells us about how our mind is organized. To bridge the gap, certain crucial questions need to be asked. Two of these questions are:

1. Why are phonological processes present in all linguistic systems?
2. What is a possible phonological process?

Much of the work in phonology of the past two decades has been centered around question 2. Phonological representations and, more generally, phonological theory bear little resemblance to the theory of classical generative phonology that I sketched in the last chapter. Phonologists have sought to characterize the set of possible phonological processes. As we have seen in the previous chapter, the theory of features and the formulation of rules in terms of natural classes are steps in that direction. Only certain groups of segments can be defined in terms of a single feature matrix. The theory says that only such groups may be involved in a phonological process. Although it is true that feature theory does provide a certain indication of the class of possible processes, it was recognized from the outset that the theory was clearly inadequate and did not offer a reliable definition of "possible process." I return to this point later in the chapter. First, I would like to discuss question 1.

Surprisingly, virtually no work in theoretical phonology has been addressed to the question of why phonological processes are present in all linguistic systems. Their existence is noted and theories are developed discussing their form and content. The question remains: What are they doing in linguistic systems? At the beginning of chapter 2, I noted that the existence of phonological processes is not a logical necessity. One could imagine a communicative system that lacked them entirely. Programming languages, which have components resembling syntax, semantics, and even morphology, have nothing that comes close to a phonological phenomenon. It is true, of course, that programming languages are not spoken and certainly do not serve the same function as natural languages. My point here is that it is conceivable that a linguistic system could have no phonological phenomena, and accordingly, the question as to why all languages have them is worth asking.

I assume if one pressed the majority of phonologists for an answer to this question, they would appeal to the fact that human languages, unlike programming languages, are spoken. By virtue of being spoken, then, languages have phonology; the raison d'être of phonological processes is phonetic. Well, what does this mean exactly? Segments may change their form depending on the context in which they occur. It seems natural to assume that these modifications render the sequence of segments easier to pronounce. They require less effort. Awkward sequences can be changed or eliminated. The total energy required is generally reduced. Referring to the examples of the previous chapter, this means that speakers of New York English say *toon* rather than *tyune* because in some sense it's easier. Arabic speakers say *an naas* 'the people' rather than *al naas* for the same reason. It is very difficult to pronounce *dog*[s] instead of *dog*[z]. However, it is my belief that the underlying motivation for phonological processes is not motivated by phonetic considerations. In the next section, I present a number of arguments against the phonetic bases of these phenomena. I argue that processing considerations (parsing) are the ultimate cause of phonological phenomena.

THE NONPHONETIC BASIS
OF PHONOLOGICAL PHENOMENA

Let's try and flesh out the idea of a phonetic motivation for phonological phenomena. From this point of view, phonological processes constitute a kind of smoothing out of the jagged edges of a phonological string. Putting together morphemes to form a word may create awkward sequences, and phonological processes are a way of dealing with such sequences. Of course, we need to get a handle on such notions as awkward sequence. One might speculate that such sequences have a higher energy cost than the output strings derived from the application of phonological processes. Phonological processes would then serve the function of reducing the total energy load involved in speech production.

A related factor is that of articulatory timing. There are certain processes that involve the displacement of a particular *articulatory gesture*, that is, the set of muscular events that are employed in the articulation of all or some aspects of a given speech sound. Such a gesture, normally associated with one segment, occurs on a neighboring segment as well. One of the most common examples of this sort involves nasal assimilation. English has a negative prefix *in-*, which may be added to adjectives and nouns. It has a number of manifestations depending on the nature of the following consonant. Some of these manifestations are illustrated in (1).

(1) active   inactive   essential   inessential
     possible   impossible   prudent   imprudent
     tangible   intangible   tolerable   intolerable
     complete   incomplete   credulous   incredulous

This negative prefix has the form *in-* before vowels and coronal stops (intangible). Before labial consonants (consonants produced by closing the lips) its form is *im-*. Notice that *m* is also a labial consonant. This difference is obvious to all. It is also reflected in English spelling (*impossible* not *inpossible*). What is less obvious but nonetheless true is that before [k] (spelled *c* in the examples) the form of the prefix also changes. The nasal consonant is not quite the same in *incomplete* as in *inactive*. The former nasal is just like the last sound (not letter) in the word *sing*. Producing this nasal involves placing the back of the tongue in contact with the soft palate (the velum). Notice that this is exactly the same gesture as that which produces the hard *c* ([k]) in *incomplete*. Sounds produced by contact with the velum are called *velars*.

To sum up, the final consonant of the negative prefix is produced as a coronal before vowels and other coronal consonants,[1] as a labial (*m*) before other labials, and as a velar before other velars. The starting point of these articulatory gestures is displaced one segment to the left and encompasses both the nasal and the following consonant. Starting from *in + possible,* the labial gesture associated with *p* begins one segment earlier. Combining *n* plus labiality yields *m* (the labial nasal). Such displacements, where the articulatory gesture associated with one segment is also associated with some adjacent segment, are called cases of *assimilation.* It might be reasoned that assimilation involves reducing the difficulty or energy load associated with a given sequence.

There is another phenomenon that will bear on this discussion: sound change. Linguistic systems are not static. They are in constant, albeit very slow, flux. Shakespearean English is comprehensible but rather different from modern English. The language of Chaucer is decipherable with the aid of a dictionary. Old English might just as well be Greek. One cannot read it without prior study. Languages undergo syntactic, semantic, morphological, lexical, and phonological changes. Phonological changes are quite similar to phonological processes. Indeed, processes are simply changes that leave a residue of alternations. These alternations provide the evidence for the incorporation of these changes into the phonological system.

One example of such change is the merger of the vowels of *caught* and *cot*. In Boston and Toronto, these words are pronounced identically. We know the vowels were historically distinct based on earlier written records and, more importantly, because they are still distinct in many English dialects. So, at some point in the history of Boston and Toronto English these two vowels were distinct. Both dialects underwent a historical change that changed the pronunciation of the vowel of *caught* to that of *cot*. Given the resemblance of processes and changes, it is natural to assume that they have similar causes. In my argumentation, I use evidence provided by both sources, that is, phonological processes and linguistic change.

I begin with a simple-minded model of phonetically motivated processes and changes. In this view, processes and changes involve reduction of energy (ease of pronunciation). If phonology works the same way as other physical systems, we would expect that phonological systems would evolve, going from a more to a less energetic state. The typical image associated with this kind of model is that of an energy well. Applying this

---

[1]Coronal liquids are a special case. Here, the nasal disappears entirely (cf. *regular–irregular, logical–illogical*).

model to the problem at hand, we would expect languages to display a marked convergence over the course of time. If each language is going toward a less energetic state, we would expect phonological systems to resemble each other more and more. In point of fact, the languages of the world display no such convergence. We have every reason to believe that the phonological systems of today are just as diverse as they were 5,000 years ago. At first glance, the phonetic theory seems to make a very wrong prediction. However, as I already stated, this is a very simple-minded model. Perhaps some crucial factor was not taken into account in my argument. Let's explore a few potential candidates.

Suppose one countered by saying that the argument is invalid because it assumes that a given process will be equally costly in energy for every language and hence for every group of speakers. There is no convergence because what is difficult or costly for one group is easier for another. Polish seems full of incredible sequences of consonants, unpronounceable by any non-Pole. Japanese speakers have a hard time distinguishing *east* from *yeast,* and asking them to pronounce the sentence *She sells sea shells by the sea shore* is an exercise in sadism. Maybe each language has its own scale of difficulty and thus its own particular evolutionary path. That's why there's no convergence.

There are a number of problems with this argument. Let us first agree that there are no significant anatomical differences insofar as our articulatory organs are concerned within the human species. We all have the same musculature for our tongue, lips, glottis, and so forth. It is therefore quite legitimate to talk about muscular effort, or energy expenditure, on a species-wide basis. In fact, there is an easy way to show that there are no differences within our species regarding linguistic behavior, be it phonological or otherwise. Any normal human infant will learn any human language; and he or she will learn it *natively.* A child born in Japan to Japanese parents is no more disposed to learn Japanese than a child born in Des Moines. If both children are raised in a Japanese-speaking environment, they will both learn Japanese with equal ease. Furthermore, there will be no way of telling which child is which purely on the basis of their speech. Language acquisition requires only that a child be exposed to the language he or she is to learn at the appropriate period. Any human language will do. The effects discussed earlier are those typical of adults, that is, of people who have already completed the language acquisition process. Language is acquired during a critical period in the child's development. Acquisition of one's native language and a second language as an adult are two, quite different things.

Given the anatomical unit of our species, it is quite difficult to define a language-specific scale of muscular effort. What would such a scale be based on? Concretely, does this mean that the reason New York English speakers say *toon* whereas London speakers say *tyune* is because *ty* requires more effort for New Yorkers than Londoners? This is absurd. It is also circular, tantamount to saying that the measure of phonetic difficulty of the sequence is determined by the presence of a process that eliminates or modifies this sequence. The argument then turns into "processes are phonetically motivated because processes are phonetically motivated. We are stuck with the fact that phonetic difficulty must be defined for our species as a whole.

A second argument might take the following form: The failure to observe convergence is not a killing blow to the phonetic hypothesis; no more so than that in the recorded history of our species, the fact that no evolutionary effects have been observed is an argument against natural selection. We simply have not been around long enough for such convergence effects to manifest themselves, but they will! After all, evolutionary changes may take hundreds of thousands or even millions of years to unfold. Our earliest written records of human language are less than 10,000 years old. Obviously, this argument is difficult to counter. There is no way of excluding the possibility that after, say, another 10,000 years, our descendants will begin to notice a marked tendency for phonological systems to converge. We are dealing with questions of probability here. This hypothesis, although possible, is certainly not the best candidate we have going for us. In addition, the existence of phonological processes is rather inconvenient. If these phenomena are supposed to exist as a manifestation of an evolutionary tendency toward minimization of articulatory effort, we don't have to wait another 10,000 years. One might argue that these processes are simply predecessors of more drastic changes to come in the future, but even this idea runs into trouble. As I have mentioned, phonologists are interested in the notion of possible process—that is, in establishing the limits of the form and substance of phonological phenomena. The results have been quite positive. There are limits to these processes. Not any imaginable change or process may occur. Even within the theory of generative phonology, the notion of natural class imposes restraints on what may and may not occur. By and large, these predictions are confirmed.[2] According to the best available evidence, what we see is what we're going to get. The sudden appearance of radically different kinds of phonological processes is squarely contrary to the results of phonological theory. It could happen, but there is no evidence that it ever will.

Finally, linguistic change is enormously rapid in evolutionary terms. The development of all the Romance languages (French, Spanish, Italian, Portuguese, etc.) from a version of Latin has taken place in less than 2,000

---

[2]As we see later, the major problem with classical generative phonology is not that it is too restrictive—that it is incapable of describing observed phenomena—but rather that it is not restrictive enough. It allows for processes generally agreed to be impossible.

years. The English of the 10th century is completely incomprehensible today. One would expect to see trends toward the lessening of muscular effort if phonological processes had a phonetic cause. No such trends appear. What we see is divergence, not convergence.

An even more telling argument against the phonetic hypothesis is the fact that certain phonological sequences modified by a process or historical change can be the final output of other processes or changes. Consider Italian. In this language, sequences of stops have been simplified to geminates: a sequence of two identical stops. This is the extreme version of an assimilatory process. The *kt* sequence in a word such as *doctor* is *dottore* in Italian. The two *t*s are pronounced. The *t* in a word such as *fatto* 'fact' is about twice as long as the one in *fato* 'fate'. The *pt* sequence becomes *tt,* as in *adottare* 'adopt', and so on. One could argue that sequences of stops involve a relatively large muscular effort; therefore, languages tend to produce processes that get rid of them. The *pt* sequence involves two articulatory gestures: a labial closure followed by a coronal closure. The result of the Italian change *tt* involves only a single gesture, the coronal one.

One would not expect that out there somewhere is another process whose effect is to produce sequences of this sort, but, of course, there are. In Moroccan Arabic, there is a process that deletes a vowel when followed by another vowel. The result of this is the *creation* of all kinds of sequences that are supposed to be more difficult to pronounce. In Classical Arabic, the presumed ancestor of Moroccan Arabic, the verbal form 'he wrote' is *kataba*. In Moroccan Arabic, the form is *ktib*.[3] We know that a vowel was originally between the *k* and the *t* because of the historical sources of Moroccan Arabic and because, even today, this vowel appears if the following vowel was deleted. The process that deletes one vowel before another applies to a phonological string from right to left. Let C be any consonant and V be any vowel. In Moroccan Arabic, a word of the form CV_1CV_2C will be pronounced CCV_2C. A word of the from CV_1CV_2CVV (VV is a long vowel) will be pronounced CV_1CCVV. In the former case, the first vowel of the word is followed by a second, V_2, and so it is deleted. In the latter case, going from right to left, V_2 is followed by the long vowel (after the intervening consonant), and so it is deleted. Now the vowel that used to follow V_1 is no longer present. It was deleted. So V_1 is pronounced providing the needed evidence for its presence. Comparison of the singular and plural forms in (2) illustrates this phenomenon.

(2) ktib   'he wrote'   kitbuu   'they wrote'

---

[3]All final short vowels were lost in Moroccan Arabic. The i is a sound similar to *e* in English *kisses*.

The derivation of the plural form proceeds as follows: the input form is *kitib + uu,* the rule of vowel deletion applies from right to left. It looks for the rightmost vowel of a form that is still followed by another vowel. The second vowel of the input form meets this description and is deleted, yielding *kit0buu,* where 0 marks the position formerly occupied by the vowel. The importance of this plural form is that it shows that there is indeed a vowel between the initial *k* and *t.* This vowel is audible in the plural form. Thus, the vowel deletion process in Moroccan Arabic acts to create in the singular form exactly the sequence that is purportedly eliminated in Italian for phonetic reasons.

A more dramatic example comes from certain Yiddish dialects. Uriel Weinreich (1958) has discussed this situation in great detail. Here, I simply present his conclusions. Yiddish, like many dialects of German, had a process that devoiced final stops and fricatives. In Standard German, for example, the word written *rad* 'wheel' is pronounced [rat]. We know this final phonetic [t] is really a *d* because when we add a suffix, it is no longer in final position and hence no longer subject to a final devoicing rule. Forms that end in a real *t* do not manifest this alternation. *t* is pronounced [t] whether it is in final position or followed by a vowel. In (3) I contrast the pronunciation of two nouns: *rad* 'wheel' and *rat* 'advice'.

(3)   *Singular*   *Plural*

rad	rat	räder
rad	rat	räte

Notice that in the singular both forms are pronounced identically. The difference in their final consonant is revealed in an inflected form such as the plural.

The rule of final devoicing is one of the most common processes in phonology. It is found in such diverse languages as Russian, Polish, Turkish, Catalan, Ojibwa (an American Indian language spoken in Ontario), and Wolof (an African language spoken in Senegal). What Weinreich noticed was that in a certain group of Yiddish dialects this process was lost. He showed convincingly that it was not the case that these dialects never had a rule of final devoicing. They did, but later on in their history this process was lost. To illustrate what this means, let's use the German example in (3). At an early period in the history of German, the two singular forms were pronounced [rad] and [rat]. At some point, the rule of final devoicing entered the language and the forms were then pronounced [rat] and [rat]. This is the case of modern German today. If modern German were ever to lose the final devoicing process, the forms would revert back to their original forms [rad] and [rat], which, of course, corresponds to their lexical representation. This is what happened in the case of the Yiddish dialects discussed by Weinreich. It is hard to reconcile this state of affairs with the phonetic theory. If processes are phonetically motivated, why should the final devoicing process suddenly disappear from the Yiddish dialects? One presumes that the same forces that purportedly motivated the process in the first place were still present in the Yiddish dialects that eventually lost it. This kind of backtracking is quite incompatible with a phonetic basis for phonological phenomena.

One might be tempted to turn to examples of biological evolution to save the phonetic theory, but this too would be a mistake. It is true that such backtracking does occur in evolution. Species may develop the ability to fly, only to lose that ability further along their evolutionary path. This is completely consistent with the theory of natural selection. Environmental conditions may change and the loss of flight would be adaptive with respect to those changes. Other adaptations may render flight unnecessary or even a disadvantage. The point is that the various evolutionary paths are shaped by natural selection. Biological changes are generated by chance (mutation), and those that work may eventually take hold in the organism. But phonological processes are not adaptive. Final devoicing is not a response to environmental conditions. It is not more useful in the mountains than by the seashore. There is no correlation whatsoever between phonological structure (or, for that matter, any aspect of linguistic structure) and the environment. Environmental conditions may be cyclic (the advance and retreat of glaciers), but there is no reasonable scenario that would tie in phonological processes to such factors. Studying the structure of a language reveals absolutely nothing about either the people who speak it or the physical environment in which they live. One must conclude that evolutionary stories will simply not work for linguistic change.

An attempt to apply the phonetic hypothesis to individuals rather than to evolutionary-type linguistic changes does not fare any better. If phonological processes are motivated as a way of reducing muscular effort, then one would expect to find correlations between the number of phonological processes and the physical state of the individual. Are phonological processes more frequent when one is tired? When one becomes old?[4] Once more, there is not a shred of evidence for any correlation of this kind.

The fact remains that all phonological processes are expressible in phonetic terms. We saw this in our discussion of the various theories of segmental representations. Phonological processes may be *expressed* in phonetic

---

[4]A physical state such as being drunk may have an effect on linguistic production. I am unaware of any systematic study of the phonology of inebriation. My feeling is that many manifestations of this condition do not correspond to phonological phenomena found in more normal situations.

terms, but this does not mean that they are *caused* by phonetic factors. It may well be the case that many (but certainly not all) phonological processes result in a reduction of muscular effort. This does not mean that reduction of muscular effort is the cause of these phenomena. Indeed, there exist phonetic effects that are doubtless genuine examples of phonetically motivated phenomena. These effects are present in all languages where the conditions for their application are met. They are not the contingent type of processes that we observe in phonological phenomena. A language or dialect may or may not have a rule of final devoicing. The phonetic effects are omnipresent, and so they are never dealt with in phonological discussions. For example, the articulation of *d* may vary according to the following vowel. The transition between *d* and *a* is different from that between *d* and *i*. This is true for all languages that have the segments *d, i,* and *a* and the sequences *di* and *da*. But it is exactly because of their omnipresence that these effects are not relevant to phonological discussion. They cannot serve to distinguish one phonological system from another and, accordingly, do not help us to characterize the notion of possible phonological system.

WHY ARE THERE PHONOLOGICAL PROCESSES? SOME SPECULATIONS

So it remains that phonological processes may be expressed phonetically without having a phonetic cause. This leaves the question of why these processes are present in all linguistic systems. I suggest that phonology makes processing possible in the form that we know it. To illustrate what I mean, try reading the following paragraph:

(4) thefactremainsthatallphonologicalprocessesareexpressibleinphone-
     tictermswesawthisinourdiscussionofthevarioustheoriesofseg-
     mentalrepresentationsphonologicalprocessesmaybeexpressedin
     phonetictermsbutthisdoesnotmeanthattheyarecausedbyphonetic
     factorsitmaywellbethecasethatmany

What you see in (4) is simply the beginning of the next to last paragraph, with all spacing and punctuation removed. I strongly doubt that many people would have the patience to read much of such a text (I hope the original text did not pose the same problem). It would be no easy task to spot a spelling error in the middle of this text. The time needed to read it is considerably longer than would be required for the same text with the proper spacing and punctuation. I therefore suggest that phonological processes fulfill a function similar to that of spacing and punctuation in written texts. To sharpen this point, let's consider the work of a syntactic parser. The objective of a parser is to take a string, usually a sentence in some language, and to produce its syntactic structure as an output. Feed the parser a sentence such as *I adore stewed prunes* and it should tell us that *I* is a noun phrase and subject of the sentence, *adore stewed prunes* is a verb phrase containing the main verb *adore* and its direct object *stewed prunes*. The construction of parsers for natural languages is a major concern of computational linguistics; they are essential for such projects as machine translation, many types of expert systems, and natural language interfaces for data bases. Questions of parsing are coming to play an ever-increasing role in the evaluation of syntactic theories.

Clearly, human beings come equipped with a parser, and part of linguistics consists of gaining an understanding of how it might work. A feature that characterizes all current work on parsing is input via a keyboard rather than a microphone. In other words, segmentation is spoon-fed to the system. Of course, this is not how it happens in oral communication, which requires analyzing a speech signal into linguistically relevant units such as sentences, phrases, words, morphemes, and ultimately sound units. Discovering how the speech signal can be so segmented is of interest to phonologists and to researchers in the area of automatic speech recognition (speak into the mike and what you say appears on the screen). It may be possible to parse sentences without word divisions and other organizational features, just as it is possible to read and understand the doctored text given earlier. In the case of reading, the task is slowed down by several orders of magnitude; what about in speech? Let me propose the following thought experiment: Suppose we removed the effects of all phonological processes from a stretch of speech. This would mean that we would take some archetypical pronunciation for each segment. This pronunciation would remain invariant in all contexts. Boundary phenomena such as final devoicing would be turned off. Stress effects, a key to the recognition of word divisions, would be leveled. It is my belief that such a stretch of speech would be incomprehensible if played back at a normal speed. If comprehensible at all, it would be necessary to slow down drastically the rate of transmission. If I am correct, phonological processes serve to facilitate parsing. It is the existence of phonological processes that makes possible the speed of oral communication that we observe in the languages of the world. Although individual phonological processes are not adaptive, it is quite possible that our current transmission rate is. Human linguistic capacity is certainly an enormous advantage to our species, doubtless essential to our survival. Would a communicative system that functioned at, say, one-fifth our speed offer the same adaptive qualities?

Many phonological processes have obvious *delimitative* effects, that is, they give information about domain boundaries (word, phase, sentence).

Stress systems are clear examples. In French, word-final syllables are stressed , that is, pronounced in a more prominent fashion than other syllables in the same word. Word divisions thus stand out quite clearly in the spoken string. They follow a stressed syllable. Hungarian stress is always found on the initial syllable of the word. Once again, word boundaries are easily detected if one knows this fact about Hungarian. Interestingly, languages almost always have their stressed syllable located near a word boundary. They may differ as to whether it is toward the beginning or the end of the word. No language places stress in the middle of the word. There is no process of the form: Given a word with n syllables, place the stress on the $n/2$th syllable, rounding to the higher number if $n/2$ is not an integer. This potential process is easily expressed and formally quite simple. It is also totally alien to human phonological systems.[5]

Many languages have harmony processes. A harmony process involves a feature whose domain is not the segment, as is usually the case, but rather a higher order constituent, such as a word. For example, in Desano, a South American Indian language spoken in Colombia and Brazil, nasalization is not a feature of a segment. It is a property of a morpheme. Morphemes are either entirely oral or entirely nasal, consonants and vowels included. Examples of consonants are *n, m,* and *ng.* Most other consonants are oral. Nasal vowels do not occur in English but are found in French: [mõ] *mon* 'my', [vẽ] *vin* 'wine', and so on. In Desano, words contain oral consonants together with oral vowels, and nasal consonants with nasal vowels. No mixing is allowed. So, [mã] is a possible Desano word and so is [ba], but both [ma] and [bã] are impossible.

Detection of morpheme or word boundaries is facilitated by the harmony process. A boundary may be placed at a change from nasal to oral or from oral to nasal. This is not 100% effective, because sometimes two oral or nasal words occur in succession. Failure to find a change of nasalization does not always imply that we are in the middle of some domain. On the other hand, changes in nasalization are fairly reliable indicators that we are at a boundary.

Certain processes are sensitive to syntactic structure and/or morphological categories. In the previous chapter, I presented a process in English whereby coronal stops followed by [y] underwent palatalization, that is, a shift in point of articulation from just behind the upper teeth to the area of the hard palate. In addition, it is the blade rather than the tip of the tongue that forms the palatal closure. This is the *ch* sound symbolized by *č*

---

[5]English stress represents a limiting case of the formal simplicity of these systems. Nevertheless, one of the achievements of modern phonology is the reduction of the English stress system to something approaching stress systems in other languages. For some discussion, see the section on the syllable later in this chapter.

This process applies most frequently to forms of the second person pronoun *you/your*.

(5) a. I know wha[č]ou want   'I know what you want'
    b. I hi[č]our brother   'I hit your brother'
    c. I wan[č]ou to leave   'I want you to leave'

In (5a), palatalization applies between the complementizer (*what*) and the subject pronoun (*you*). In (5b), this rule applies within a verb phrase. The final consonant of the verb *hit* is palatalized by the initial [y] of the possessive pronoun of its object. The final consonant of the verb in (5c) is palatalized by the object pronoun *you*.[6] If we replace the pronoun by a noun beginning with the same sound, palatalization becomes more difficult, if not downright impossible.[7]

(6) a. I know what Eunice wants   *I know wha[č]Eunice
    b. I hit Yorick   wants
    c. I want universal freedom   *I hi[č]orick
                                          *I wan[č]universal freedom

Speakers of English should feel a clear contrast between the sentences of (5) and those of (6). It is possible that the special phonological behavior of the second person pronoun has implications for parsing strategies.

The Quebec French process that transforms *t* and *d* into [t^s] and [d^z], respectively, before the vowels [i] and [ü] (its technical name is *affrication*) may also indicate word boundary sites. This process applies without exception within the word and may even be observed in the pronunciation of English words as part of a Quebec accent. This does not mean that Quebec French speakers are incapable of producing the sequences [ti], [tü], [di], and [ü], as the following pair of forms shows:

(7) a. [pasãt^{s}ünik] (il n'est) pas sans tunique 'he is not without a tunic'
    b. [pasãtünik] (une) passante unique 'a solitary female passerby'

I have transcribed both forms without indicating the word boundaries. This reflects the real-life situation. French speakers (or speakers of any other

---

[6]Technically speaking, *you* is the subject of a subordinate clause. This is without consequence for our discussion.

[7]The asterisk preceding the sentences to the right indicates that they are ill formed.

language for that matter) do not normally pause between words.[8] Even without the word boundaries, the sequence [tü] rather than [tˢü] is surefire proof that a boundary exists between these two segments, and this is precisely the sequence that straddles the words *passante* and *unique*.

Clearly, a single process such as Quebec French affrication cannot give clues for every word boundary. It can only be effective for sequences of the type "coronal stop plus high front vowel." Languages typically have a fair number of different phonological phenomena. Collectively, they may well supply clues for a substantial number of divisions; enough at least to give the parser a fighting chance to do its work in the allotted time. To sum up, I suggest here that although phonological processes are expressed in phonetic terms, they do not have underlying phonetic motivation. On the other hand, there does seem to be some evidence that they play an important role in parsing. Specifically, they provide important cues as to the number and location of constituent boundaries. Such information, as we have seen, is vital for syntactic processing to take place at the observed transmission rate of oral speech. One might wonder why demarcative cues are not constant across languages.

Why do languages utilize such a wide variety of different processes to accomplish this function? Why aren't phonetic cues for constituent boundaries simply hard wired into our brains? Any answer to these questions will necessarily involve a good deal of speculation, and they actually go much deeper: They are related to the question of why our species employs a variety of different linguistic systems—why there are many human languages. Languages differ not only in their phonology but in their syntax and morphology as well. Why isn't our entire linguistic system completely predefined? The ultimate answers to these questions will be a while in coming. In the meantime, we can certainly begin to consider various possibilities. Moreover, recent advances in phonological theory (and, of course, all other areas of linguistic theory) hold out the promise of setting us off in the right direction.

Theoretical developments of the last 10 years make one fact quite clear: We have vastly overestimated the extent to which linguistic systems vary. There is a hard core of linguistic structure that is common to all human languages. It is natural to assume that we are born with this hard core

---

[8]Indeed, there is a process in French called *enchaînement,* whereby a final consonant of one word may form the syllable-initial consonant of a following word that begins with a vowel. This process may result in ambiguity, as in the case of the pair, *trop unis* 'too united' and *trop puni* 'punished too much'. Both these forms may be pronounced [tropüni]. Significantly, many French speakers pronounce the first form [troüni]. The point is that the *p,* when it is pronounced, forms a syllable with the following *ü.* There is no pause between the words.

(linguists call it *universal grammar* or UG). Learning one's native language involves fleshing out UG, picking out of the linguistic environment those aspects of the input data that characterize the language that is being acquired. This language-specific part may be very large or very small with respect to UG. UG might contain only the most basic ingredients of human language: It is oral, there are words, syntactic processes are defined in terms of categories rather than linear position within a string (sentence), and so on. Everything else could be language-specific and, thus, must make up the part of linguistic structure that is learned. It turns out that this is not the case. Linguists are discovering that UG forms a rather large part of the total grammar of a language. Furthermore, the direction that our theoretical advances are taking us is one of an ever-increasing role for UG. The idea that our linguistic system is hard wired into our brain is not that far off the mark. From our point of view as English speakers, a language such as Chinese might seem totally different from our own. In fact, these two languages as well as all other human languages are nearly identical. The differences that seem all important to us are relatively minor. When one considers to what extent systems as complex as languages could vary, the small variations that one finds between the grammar of one language and that of another are relatively unimportant. Furthermore, the observed differences in linguistic systems are anything but random.

Languages differ along well-defined lines called parameters. A parameter may be thought of as a kind of a switch. Typically, this switch has two positions: on or off. A particular property, be it syntactic, morphological, or phonological, may be present or absent from a system, or it may take one of two possible forms,. Language acquisition may now be defined as determining just what the particular settings are for the series of switches appropriate to what is being learned. One may think of human linguistic capacity as a great printer with a series of dip switches under its cover. Going from English to Chinese to Navajo to Swahili is simply a question of changing the setting of these switches.

Let me give one example from phonology to illustrate this point. Phonological segments are grouped together in constituents called syllables. The relevance of syllables to phonology is discussed later in this chapter. For now, just assume they exist. A syllable consists of two components. There are one or more consonants at the beginning. This is the *onset* of the syllable. The second component contains the vowel and possibly a following consonant, provided that the latter is part of the same syllable. A vowel with an optionally occurring consonant is called the *rime* of the syllable. The vowel itself, which is the main part of the syllable, is called the *nucleus*. Syllable structure can be easily described using a tree diagram. I use the labels *S* for syllable, *O* for onset, *R* for rime, and *N* for nucleus. The *x*s represent the positions in which the various segments (consonants or vowels) can occur.

(8) *Syllable Structure*

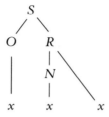

Each constituent dominates a single position (*x*) in (8). As we shall see, constituents may dominate more than one segment. Applying this structure to the syllables *pa* and *pat* gives the representations shown in (9).

(9)

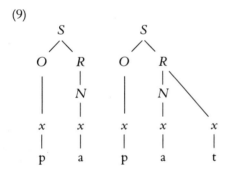

Now, the question is, if we take all the languages in the world, how many syllable types must we allow for? The answer is surprising. Three parameters suffice to define every extant syllable type. Furthermore, there is a dependence among these three parameters. They are:

(10) 1. Does the rime branch?   [no/yes]
      2. Does the nucleus branch?   [no/yes]
      3. Does the onset branch?   [no/yes]

A constituent that branches contains more than one member. For example, a branching onset would have the form given in (11).

(11)

(11) represents the onset of a syllable such as *play*. One might wonder about the maximum number of consonants that can fit into an onset. We have already seen examples with one and two. How high can we go? Can we find languages with, say, 14 consonants in an onset? Or 5? Or 3? The answer is no. Onsets can have a maximum of two positions.[9] The same is true for the other syllabic constituents, rime and nucleus. They may have one member (nonbranching) or two (branching).

We are now in a position to define, based on (10), the syllable systems of all human languages. First, it should be made clear that languages, like cars, come with certain standard equipment—syllable types that are present in every language. The possibilities in (10) represent the optional features. So, every language has the full series of nonbranching constituents. What distinguishes the syllable systems of different languages is whether or not they permit branching constituents. We can now express the possible syllable inventories in terms of a three-digit binary number. This is in keeping with our assumption that linguistic differences are expressed in terms of differing (binary) parameter settings. So, for each of the three parameters in (10), let 0 equal a *no* and 1 equal a *yes*. The number 000 defines a system, or class, of syllables, where neither the rime, the nucleus, nor the onset may branch. 111 defines the case where all three constituents may branch. This gives us the eight possibilities given in (12).

(12) a. 000   b. 100   c. 110   d. 101   e. 111
       f. 010   g. 001   h. 011

---

[9]Some languages contain forms that would appear to contradict this statement. The word *string* in English begins with a sequence of three consonants. I remind the reader again that I am talking about phonological segments here and not letters. The syllable theory that I am describing predicts that the sequence *str* cannot form an onset. It has too many segments. What makes the study of phonological phenomena interesting is to show that indeed *str* does not form an onset. In fact, no sequence of *s* + *consonant* forms an onset. The fact that *str* has three segments is really a red herring. What is important is that *s* followed by even a single consonant does not form an onset. I present the evidence for all this in a later chapter.

Languages may be found that represent the parameter settings of the first row. The cases (12f–h) do not appear to exist. In concrete terms, a branching rime represents a closed syllable—a syllable ending in a consonant. A branching nucleus represents a long vowel or a heavy diphthong—the sort that we find in English words such as *see, buy, boy, out,* and so on. Languages illustrating the first five syllable inventories are given in (13).

(13) a. 000   No branching rimes, nuclei, or onsets: *Desano*
      b. 100   Branching rimes, but no branching nuclei or onsets: *Quechua*
      c. 100   Branching rimes and nuclei, no branching onsets: *Arabic*
      d. 101   Branching rimes and onsets, no branching nuclei: *Spanish*
      e. 111   Branching rimes, nuclei, and onsets: *English*

As already mentioned, the systems (12f–h) do not exist. Their absence means that the three parameters are not entirely independent of one another. The following implication holds: If branching rimes are excluded from the syllabic inventory of a language, branching nuclei and branching onsets are likewise excluded.[10] In terms of our binary number system, this means that if the leftmost digit of the binary number is 0, the other two digits must likewise be 0. In acquisition terms, it implies that one doesn't even bother with the two other parameters if the first is set to 0.

If the model given in (10) is correct, setting three parameters is all that is required to learn the syllable inventory of one's language. The seemingly endless variety of syllable systems is reduced to three binary choices, two of which are dependent on the other. All this is very similar to buying a new car. One goes to the dealer and specifies a certain number of parameters: the color, manual or automatic, radio or no radio, and so forth. It would be rather strange to tell the car salesperson, "I'd like a nice car with a motor, four wheels, headlights, brakes, and a steering wheel." These things form part of the car's universal grammar. We don't need to talk about them. They are all part of what it means to be a car. In the same way, a child does not need to learn that his or her language has nonbranching rimes, nuclei,

---

[10]Certain aspects of this statement are controversial. The absence of closed syllables (i.e., no branching rimes) clearly implies the absence of branching onsets. We can certainly eliminate systems 001 and 011. There are a number of cases in the literature of languages having the system 010—no branching rimes or onsets but branching nuclei. Such a language would have only open syllables but would have long vowels or heavy diphthongs. For some purported cases of 010 languages, the so-called long vowels may well be analyzable as sequences of two distinct nuclei rather than as a single branching nucleus. This difference is roughly that of the difference between *hyena* and *diner* in English. The former word has a sequence of two nuclei, the latter, a single heavy diphthong. If I am correct, purported cases of 010 would all involve nuclear sequences. In reality, then, they would be 000 languages.

and onsets. That's standard equipment. This standard equipment comprises that vast bulk of a linguistic system. Going back to our syllable example, all the details of the constituents, their internal organization, their interface with phonological processes, are part of our standard equipment. What must be learned are the three options that define the particular syllable inventory that characterizes the language being acquired. So, what linguists are trying to do is find out what aspects of linguistic structure are the standard equipment and what options (parameters) are available to the learner. Syllable structure is, of course, but a small part of the total picture. The expectation is that under analysis, all aspects of linguistic structure may be similarly resolved. It is in this context that we turn to the second question that was posed at the beginning of this chapter: What is a possible phonological process? The search for the answer to this question has caused phonological theory to undergo dramatic changes from the model of classical generative phonology described in the previous chapter.

THE RECENT EVOLUTION
OF PHONOLOGICAL THEORY

The seminal work on classical generative phonology is *The sound pattern of English* (SPE) by Noam Chomsky and Morris Halle (Chomsky & Halle, 1968). The fundamental principles of generative phonology described in chapter 2 are taken from this source. The book is truly a remarkable document for a number of reasons. It is the cornerstone of phonological research of the past 20 years. It set out in painstaking detail the formal structure of a phonological theory. But then in the final chapter, after 400 pages, the authors note that the theory has some very serious flaws. So SPE simultaneously produced the clearest expression of a phonological theory yet to appear in print as well as a list of problems associated with the theory that has preoccupied phonologists ever since. What was so wrong with the theory?

Chomsky and Halle demanded more of their theory than a formalism for expressing phonological processes. They wanted their theory to be able to distinguish a commonplace phenomenon, such as final devoicing or palatalization, from one that was much more unlikely or even impossible. Chomsky and Halle wanted this distinction to be reflected in the formal expression of these processes. And so they proposed an evaluation metric— a way of ranking processes according to their naturalness. The naturalness of a process (or rule, as they called it) was in inverse proportion to the number of features needed to express it. Rules that required more features were ranked lower on the naturalness scale. Rules that required fewer features should be quite common. Let me give one example of what they meant. The formal expression of the final devoicing process looks like (14).

(14) *Final Devoicing*
    $[-\text{sonorant}] \rightarrow [-\text{voice}]/\underline{\hspace{2em}}\#$

This is the formalism of the final devoicing process that I discussed earlier in conjunction with German and Yiddish. [−sonorant] defines the class of stops and fricatives. Notice that we needn't (and indeed mustn't) include [+voice] in the input matrix of this rule. If the rule applies to a voiceless nonsonorant, it won't do any harm. The application will be vacuous because a voiceless nonsonorant is already voiceless and changing it to [−voice] doesn't change it at all. In such cases, the output form is identical to the input form. This is just as if the rule did not apply at all. That is why we need not include the specification [+voice] in our matrix that defines the class of segments to undergo the rule. We must not include it because we have an evaluation metric that will rate the naturalness of this rule according to the number of features in its formal expression. Including features that are not absolutely necessary will cause this metric to incorrectly evaluate this rule. The sharp symbol # in the right context of this rule indicates a word boundary. Summing up, this rule states that any obstruent, a stop or fricative sound, occurring in word-final position will be voiceless—a fair statement of the facts. The evaluation metric will assign a naturalness rating of 3 to this rule. The word boundary # counts as one feature. So, this is a pretty natural rule, and as indicated previously, it is found commonly in a wide variety of languages.

Thus, the theory predicts that rule (14) should be more natural than a more restricted one—say, one that devoices only labial stops, such as *p,* rather than any stop at all. This is certainly true. For the moment, the only cloud on the horizon is the fact that even very improbable rules, such as the one I just described, would receive a rating that does not seem very high (low in naturalness). To my knowledge, a process of devoicing that is restricted to labials has never been attested. One would perhaps be happier if such a rule were rated much less natural than it is. Be that as it may, the evaluation metric appears to predict the facts in a fair number of cases. Many natural processes are expressed with less features than their unnatural counterparts.

Closer scrutiny of the evaluation metric reveals a number of rather serious problems. Chomsky and Halle note some of them. The first problem involves the relationship between the input set and the structural changes it undergoes. In the formalism developed in SPE, there is no apparent connection between these two classes. This results in very wrong predictions in a substantial number of cases. Here is one example. In many languages, the velar stops, *k* and *g,* are palatalized before front (i.e., [−back]) vowels. They become *č* and *ǰ,* respectively. [č] represents a sound similar to *ch,* as in *church;* [ǰ], the sounds spelled *j* and *dg,* as in *judge.* We can illustrate this process with an example from Italian.

(15) ami[k]o 'friend'   ami[č]i 'friends'

The [k] of the singular form is transformed into [č] when followed by the masculine plural suffix *-i.* The formal expression of this process is given in (16).[11]

(16) *Velar Palatalization*

$$
\begin{bmatrix} -\text{sonorant} \\ -\text{anterior} \end{bmatrix} \rightarrow \begin{bmatrix} -\text{back} \\ +\text{coronal} \\ +\text{delayed release} \\ +\text{strident} \end{bmatrix} / \underline{\hspace{1cm}} \begin{bmatrix} -\text{cons} \\ -\text{back} \end{bmatrix}
$$

First of all, it takes a hefty eight features to express this very frequently occurring process. In contrast, our mythical rule of final devoicing restricted to labials would only take five features! If labial devoicing with a rating of five is unnatural, then velar palatalization, rated eight, should be truly extraterrestrial. In fact, it is quite banal, occurring in such languages as Italian, James Bay Cree (a Canadian Indian language spoken in Ontario and Quebec), Acadian French, and so on. What is worse, however, is that it is no more costly (in terms of features) to express the inverse of this process, that is, a hypothetical process whereby palatal consonants become velars before front vowels. This is an unfortunate result because there exist no known cases of such a process. The conclusions are quite troubling: The very natural rule of velar palatalization is as costly as its unattested inverse. Something is clearly wrong here.

This suggests a quite general problem. One can take any phonological rule and either change the value of a particular feature or change a feature mentioned in the rule for another. The result is almost inevitably gibberish—a process never observed in any phonological system. Let's start with our rule of final devoicing (the real one) formulated in (14) and repeated here for convenience.

(17) *Final Devoicing*
[−sonorant] → [−voice] / _____#

---

[11]I will spare the reader the definitions of all the features involved in this rule. One can take it on faith that they are indeed necessary to express this process.

Starting with (17) we can make some very minor changes; changes that do not effect the evaluation of the resulting rule with respect to the original version. The theory predicts that all such processes should be equally likely (natural).

Variations on Rule (17)

  a. [+sonorant] → [−voice] / _____#
  b. [−sonorant] → [+voice] / _____#
  c. [−sonorant] → [−voice] / #_____
  d. [−sonorant] → [+nasal] / _____#
  e. [−coronal] → [−voice] / _____#
  f. [−sonorant] → [−voice] / _____[+coronal]

I have made some minimal changes to rule (17). In each case, our feature count is identical, and the theory predicts that processes (a–f) should be as likely to occur as (17). I briefly describe the effects of these strange processes as follows: Rule (a) states that sonorants, that is, vowels, liquids, and nasals, are devoiced in word-final position. It is possible to find voiceless resonants, but any process that produces them is not limited to the class of resonants. Such processes effect nonresonants as well.[12] Rule (b) voices nonsonorants in final position. If this process exists at all (it has been reported in Dakota, an American Indian language), it is excessively rare. The third rule, (c), devoices nonsonorants in initial position. I have observed a process that looks something like this in Lac Simon Algonkin, a language spoken in Northern Quebec. The analysis is problematic, and it is not obvious that (c) expresses the correct generalization. Be that as it may, (c), like (b), is much rarer than the final devoicing process.

In the first three processes of (17) I have simply changed the value of one feature or changed the position of the context from right to left. Each new rule results in a drastic drop in naturalness. Rules (a–c) are quite rare, if not downright impossible. Things get even worse when we start playing with the features themselves. Rule (d) says that nonsonorants become nasals at the ends of words. Some nonsonorants can certainly become nasals, but word-final position is not the context where this can occur. Furthermore, a nasalization process does not effect all of the nonsonorants, only a certain subset of them. In Desano and in Quebec French, voiced stops become nasal in a nasal environment. In Korean, neutral (neither tense nor aspirated) stops become nasals when followed by a nasal consonant. Rule (d) is not attested. Rule (e) says that noncoronals devoice in final position. The set of

---

[12]Southern Paiute, an American Indian language described by Edward Sapir, has a devoicing process that effects final syllables among other things. This process is significantly different from (17a) however.

noncoronals includes all vowels and labial, velar, and palatal consonants. No process has ever been shown to affect this class in any way whatsoever. Finally, rule (f) says that nonsonorants devoice before coronal consonants. This rule would change the sequence *bt* into *pt*, which is reasonable. It would also change *bd* into *pd* and leave *gp* unchanged (*p* being a noncoronal consonant), which is not at all reasonable.

Examples of this sort can be formulated for any rule one cares to write. Chomsky and Halle were quite aware of this problem. Their analysis of the situation was that the theory was too formal. In a given process or in a given representation, every feature was equivalent to every other feature. The remedy proposed by the two authors was to take into account the intrinsic value of the features. Certain combinations of features were natural, whereas others were rare or impossible. Any evaluation metric should take these factors into account. The germ of a solution came from work done 30 years earlier by a linguist (and prince) who was a member of the celebrated Prague School, active before the second world war (cf. Trubetzkoy, 1958). This was the theory of *markedness,* which the authors adapted to the theory of generative phonology.

The Theory of Markedness

Chomsky and Halle were trying to construct a theory that did more than represent various observations about phonological systems in a concise manner. Their objective was to create a phonological theory whose expressive power was closely correlated to the probability of a given segment or a given process showing up in some system. Their theory contained an evaluation metric whose purpose was to reflect these kinds of correlations. This evaluation metric was theory-specific, feeding off the kinds of phonological representations found in SPE. As we have seen, this metric was fraught with difficulties, giving clearly wrong results in a large number of very obvious cases. Chomsky and Halle were, of course, aware of these problems. Their solution was to tinker with the nature of the phonological representations expressible in their theory. The evaluation metric remains unchanged: Natural or likely processes or segments should be more highly valued by the metric than improbable or unnatural ones. To see how their proposal works, we must enter into a somewhat technical discussion. It should be borne in mind that a markedness theory is only expressible with respect to some theory of phonological representations (such as that of SPE).

It has been known for some time that certain feature specifications display a definite predilection for other feature specifications. That is, the value of one feature may have an impact on the value of another. The theory of markedness, presented in the final chapter of SPE, was an attempt to formalize these affiliations among features. Examples are not hard to come by. Let's consider vowels. The following vowels are common (but not ubiquitous):[13]

(18) i   u
      e   o

What distinguishes the vowels in the left column from those in the right? We have already seen that the left column contains vowels that are [−back]. The vowels of the right column are [+back]. But there is more. Both back vowels are also characterized by lip rounding. Not surprisingly, we call this feature [round]. Thus, *i* and *e* are [−round], *u* and *o* are [+round]. The rounding of the back vowels is not some automatic phonetic consequence of the rest of their articulation. These features are subject to phonological control. In fact, all four logical possibilities involving the features [back] and [round] occur. Turkish is a language with four [+high] vowels.

(19) *The Turkish High Vowels*

$$
\begin{bmatrix} -\text{back} \\ -\text{round} \end{bmatrix} \quad \begin{bmatrix} -\text{back} \\ +\text{round} \end{bmatrix} \quad \begin{bmatrix} +\text{back} \\ -\text{round} \end{bmatrix} \quad \begin{bmatrix} +\text{back} \\ +\text{round} \end{bmatrix}
$$

        i   ü   ɨ   u

i and *u* have rough equivalents in English. *ü* is the French *u* as in *tu*. *ɨ* exists as a reduced vowel in English. We find it as the final vowel in words like *kisses* and *George's*. Now, the fact is that not all of these four vowels are equally common. It is easy to find languages that have *i* and *u* but not *ü* or *ɨ* (Spanish and Arabic are two examples). What we never find, however, is a language that has *ü* without having *i* (French has both) or *ɨ* without having *u* (Russian has both). What this means is that there is a correlation between the features [back] and [round]. In the normal case (what we can now call the *unmarked* case), these features have the same value. We can represent this fact by using a variable α, which ranges over + and −. An unmarked vowel is thus:

(20) $\begin{bmatrix} \alpha\text{back} \\ \alpha\text{round} \\ -\text{low} \end{bmatrix}$

---

[13]These vowels are pronounced roughly as follows:
  i   as in *feet*
  e   as in *wait*
  u   as in *boot*
  o   as in *soak*

I include the specification [−low] to exclude the vowel *a*, which is [+low] from consideration. This vowel behaves differently with respect to the features [back] and [round]. The matrix (20), when applied to vowels, will specify the set {*i*, *e*, *u*, *o*}. These are the vowels that are either [−back, −round] (when α = −) or [+back, +round] (when α = +). The way of specifying the more marked series {ü, ö, ɨ, ʌ}[14] is with the variable −α. This variable also ranges over + and −. It has a value opposite to that of α occurring in the same expression.

$$(21) \quad \begin{bmatrix} \alpha \text{back} \\ -\alpha \text{round} \\ -\text{low} \end{bmatrix}$$

So, (20) represents the natural state of affairs with respect to nonlow vowels. (21) is the more marked condition. Chomsky and Halle incorporated a series of these sorts of expression into phonological theory. They took the form of conventions that resembled phonological rules but that played a very different role. They called these *marking conventions*. Their function is to state what the normal or expected value of a feature is according to the context (the other features in its matrix) in which it occurred. We can think of unmarked values of features as their default values. In other words, a nonlow, back vowel is normally round (as are *u* and *o*). So, the unmarked or default value for the feature [round] is [+round] for vowels that are both back and nonlow. A marking convention for the feature [round] is given in (22).

(22) *Marking Convention [round]*

$$[\text{u round}] \rightarrow [\alpha \text{round}] / \begin{bmatrix} \alpha \text{back} \\ -\text{low} \end{bmatrix}$$

To complete the picture, Chomsky and Halle changed the form of lexical representations. Instead of having columns of feature specifications containing +s and −s, a specification was either absent or present. The absence of a specification for a feature meant that its unmarked or expected value was called for. The specification [m F], for some feature F, indicated that the marked value of the feature F was required. What this value was (+ or −) could be discovered by applying the relevant marking convention, such as (22). The function of the marking convention is to translate the specifica-

---

[14]The vowel *ö* is a rounded *e*, as in French *feu*. The vowel ʌ is an unrounded *o* (a vowel just like *o* but with no lip rounding), as in English *cut*.

tions blank (written *u* in the convention) and *m* into the familiar +s and −s. The end result was a completely specified feature matrix where each feature was preceded by either + or −.

To see how this works, let us consider the representations of the vowels {*i, u, e, o, a*}. (23) gives their definition in terms of the features [high], [back], [round], and [low].

(23)

	High	Back	Round	Low
i	+	−	−	−
u	+	+	+	−
e	−	−	−	−
o	−	+	+	−
a	−	+	−	+

The version of (23) reflecting the markedness values for these features is presented in (24).

(24)

	High	Back	Round	Low
i		−		
u		+		
e	m	−		
o	m	+		
a				

To convert the representations of (24) into those of (23), we need some other marking conventions in addition to (22).

(25) a. [u low] → i. [+low] / [_____, u back, u round]
          ii. [−low]
      b. [u high] → [+high]
      c. [u back] → [+back]/ [_____, +low]
      d. i. = (22)
          ii. [u round] → [−round] / [_____, +low]

In addition to the four marking conventions, there are two redundancy rules. Unlike the marking conventions, these rules allow for no marked situations. They are conditions of well formedness for phonological matrices and brook no exceptions.

(26) [+low] → [−high]
      [+high] → [−low]

It is easy to see why (26) must be true. The feature [high] refers to segments involving the raising of the body of the tongue toward the roof of the mouth. The feature [low] involves the lowering of this same organ. Because we are born with only one tongue, it is impossible to simultaneously raise it and lower it. Therefore, no segment can be specified [+low, +high], which explains the well-formedness conditions in (26).

The reader will note that four specifications appear in (24): blank, m, + and −. The evaluation metric counts the latter three specifications as one unit of cost. The blank (absence of specification) has no cost. We can apply the conventions (25) to the grid (24) with the expected result being (23). The conventions apply in the order in which they appear. The well-formedness conventions (26) apply at any point in which their structural condition is satisfied. (25ai) applies first to the only segment which is not marked for the features [back] and [round], a. (25aii) is the default case. In all contexts other than a matrix unmarked for [back] and [round], the unmarked value for the feature [low] is [−low]. The matrices in (27) show the results of applying (25ai−ii) to (24).

(27) *Representations following (25a)*

	High	Back	Round	Low
i		−		−
u		+		−
e	m	−		−
o	m	+		−
a				+

The context for the redundancy rule (26) is now met in the case of *a*, and it applies.

(28) *The Application of (26)*

	High	Back	Round	Low
i		−		−
u		+		−
e	m	−		−
o	m	+		−
a	−			+

Next, convention (25b) applies, filling in the feature values of [high] for *i* and *u*. Note that this convention cannot apply to *a* because its value for this feature has already been specified. The convention has no memory and cannot know that the lexical representation of *a* was unmarked for the feature [high].

(29) *Application of (25b)*

	High	Back	Round	Low
i	+	−		−
u	+	+		−
e	*m*	−		−
o	*m*	+		−
a	−			+

Because *e* and *o* are marked for the feature [high], they receive the value − for this feature, that is, the opposite of its unmarked value.

(30) *Application of (25b): − Marked Value*

	High	Back	Round	Low
i	+	−		−
u	+	+		−
e	−	−		−
o	−	+		−
a	−			+

Convention (25c) now applies to supply the specification for the feature [back]. *a* is the only segment not yet specified for this feature. It is specified as [+low], thus the unmarked value of this feature is [+back].

(31) *Application of (25c)*

	High	Back	Round	Low
i	+	−		−
u	+	+		−
e	−	−		−
o	−	+		−
a	−	+		+

All that remains now is to fill in the values for the feature [round]. Convention (25di) applies to the first four vowels. The unmarked case is for the feature [round] to agree with the feature [back]. (25dii) applies only to low vowels. In this case, the unmarked value for [round] is [−round]. This case applies to *a*.

(32) *Application of (25d)*

	High	Back	Round	Low
i	+	−	−	−
u	+	+	+	−
e	−	−	−	−
o	−	+	+	−
a	−	+	−	+

With the help of the marking conventions (25) and the redundancy rules (26), we have succeeded in deriving the completely specified (23) from the partially specified (24).

Now, if only marked values are counted by the evaluation metric, markedness theory gives us a way of solving some of the cases where the theory makes wrong predictions. First of all, it is now possible to capture the fact that the vowels *i* and *u* are more natural (less marked) than *ü* or *ɨ*. The lexical representations of all four vowels are presented in (33).

(33)	High	Back	Round	Low
i		−		
u		+		
ü		−	m	
ɨ		+	m	

A glance at (33) shows that the formal representation of these vowels cor-rectly represents their degree of naturalness—their likeliness of occurrence in a given vowel system. The unmarked case is for nonlow vowels to agree in backness and roundness. It is possible but less likely to find the other combinations of these two features. This is what the theory of markedness is all about.

By taking into account the intrinsic nature of phonological features, it is possible to distinguish the most common segments from those that are least common. What about phonological processes? The problems of the original theory centered around them. Chomsky and Halle showed that it is possible to use the same conventions that apply to phonological segments for im-proving the results given by the evaluation metric. To see how this works, let's consider a very simple example. Suppose there exists a process that fronts vowels in some context. Given a *u* as an input, what is the expected outcome of this process? Experience teaches us that the fronted version of *u* is more likely to be *i* than *ü*. The problem is that two features separate *u* from *i*, whereas only one separates *u* from *ü*. The formal expression of these two rules is given in (34).

(34) a. $u \to i$

$$\begin{bmatrix} +\text{high} \\ +\text{back} \\ +\text{syll} \end{bmatrix} \to \begin{bmatrix} -\text{back} \\ -\text{round} \end{bmatrix} / \text{in some context}$$

b. $u \to ü$

$$\begin{bmatrix} +\text{high} \\ +\text{back} \\ +\text{syll} \end{bmatrix} \to [-\text{back}] / \text{in some context}$$

In the original version of the theory, the structural change to take us from *u* to *i* costs two features, [back] and [round]. On the other hand, $i \to ü$ only requires one feature to be changed. Both processes are possible, but (34a) is supposed to be more likely than (34b). Thus, we need another way of representing these processes so that we get the right results—(34b) should be more costly than (34a). Chomsky and Halle introduced a notion that they called *linking*. Linking works in the following way: Every time a phonological rule is applied, we check the structural changes brought about by the rule in question. If these changes match the structural description of a marking convention, then this convention is also applied. This sounds more complicated than it is in practice. Let's consider the new formulation of the rule $u \to i$. It is shown in (35).

(35) $u \to i$ *(New Version)*

$$\begin{bmatrix} +\text{high} \\ +\text{back} \\ +\text{syll} \end{bmatrix} \to [-\text{back}] / \text{in some context}$$

Rule (35) applies to some *u* and changes its feature [back] from + to −. We now check the marking conventions (25) to see if we have some new grist for their mill. Indeed, convention (25di), repeated as (36) for convenience, is sensitive to the feature [back]—the one we just changed. Furthermore, because its specification is [αback] in the convention, either [+back] or [−back] in combination with [−low] will satisfy the input conditions of this convention.

(36) = (25di)

$$[\text{u round}] \to [\text{αround}]/ \begin{bmatrix} \text{αback} \\ -\text{low} \end{bmatrix}$$

u is [+high] and therefore [−low], and we have just changed its value for the feature [back]. This means that according to the linking procedure we must now apply (36). This convention will determine the value of [round] in function of the value of [back]. Because u has been changed to [−back], (36) will also change it to [−round], and voilà, we have derived an i. This means that we no longer need to specify the value of [round] in the rule $u \rightarrow i$. The convention (36) will do this via linking.

But now another very reasonable question arises. What do we do if we really want to only change [back] and not [round]? The process $u \rightarrow \ddot{u}$ does exist. How can we represent it? Chomsky and Halle proposed a further refinement to linking:

(37) A marking convention that interprets a feature [F] may not link to a rule whose structural change includes [F].

If we want to front a u without also rounding it, we need only mention its feature [+round] in the matrix to the right of the arrow, as shown in (38).

(38) a. u → ü
     (new version) $$\begin{bmatrix} +high \\ +back \\ +syll \end{bmatrix} \rightarrow \begin{bmatrix} -back \\ +round \end{bmatrix} / \text{ in some context}$$

It may seem paradoxical to mention [+round] in the structural *change* of (38); u is already round before the application of this rule. This specification is crucial, however. It is what turns off the subsequent linking of rule (38) with convention (36). The feature [round] is affected neither by the rule nor the convention. The only real change that takes place concerns the feature [back]. Even better, rule (38) is now more costly than rule (35). This corresponds to the desired results given the greater likelihood of the latter process.

The theory of markedness has improved on the original theory in two areas: It permits us to distinguish between more and less likely segments, and it ranks phonological processes along the scale of complexity in a more realistic fashion. Generative phonology with this theory of markedness is clearly superior to what we had before. But the problems are far from over.

Enter the Syllable

Generative phonology, in addition to the formal mechanisms already described, came equipped with a series of abbreviatory devices.[15] These devices were designed to work in concert with the evaluation metric to enable one to distinguish natural contexts from unnatural ones. Consider a rule that stresses a final syllable (such as French).[16] As we have seen, words may end in vowels or a certain number of consonants. Word-final position is

---

[15]In this section, I very roughly follow the line of argumentation presented in Kahn (1976).

[16]We see in a later section that stress assignment is no longer handled by rules of the SPE sort.

indicated by the boundary marker #. How can we then express this process? Suppose our language has open and closed syllables and that there is a maximum of one word-final consonant. We will use the specification [+stress] to indicate that a vowel (i.e., a member of the set [+syll], where *syll* stands for syllabic) bears stress. The rule of final stressing is formulated in (39).

(39) *Final Stressing*

$$[+\text{syll}] \rightarrow [+\text{stress}] \left\{ \begin{array}{ll} / \underline{\hspace{1cm}} \# & \text{i.} \\ / \underline{\hspace{1cm}} [-\text{syll}] \# & \text{ii.} \end{array} \right\}$$

We are required to mention two contexts for this rule: (a) the case where the final vowel is in an open syllable and thus occurs immediately before a word boundary, and (b) the case where the final vowel is in a closed syllable and so a consonant ([−syll]) intervenes between the final vowel and the word boundary. It seems unreasonable to treat these two contexts as if they were totally different. In fact, what is important is that the vowel is the *final* vowel of the word. It makes no difference whether a consonant intervenes or not. What we really want to say is that a vowel is stressed if it is followed by a word boundary, with the possibility of an intervening consonant. The presence of this consonant is optional. It has no real bearing on the rule. In classical generative phonology, the way to indicate optional elements in the context of a rule is to put them between parentheses. This allows us to collapse the two contexts of rule (39) into the single context of rule (40).

(40) *Final Stressing (New Version)*
$$[+\text{syll}] \rightarrow [+\text{stress}] / \underline{\hspace{1cm}}([-\text{syll}])\#$$

The parentheses notation was generally accepted and caused no particular controversy. There was another abbreviatory device that raised many more hackles: the curly brackets.[17] Curly brackets are used to combine disparate elements into a single rule context.

(41) *Curly Brackets*
$$A \rightarrow B / \{C, D, E, F \ldots \}$$

(41) means that segments that are members of the set A undergo the change B in the context C or D or E or F or . . . . The problem was that no logical relation need be present between the various members of this expression. Here's one example. To return to New York English, it is a commonly

---

[17]To my knowledge, the linguist James McCawley was the first to point an accusing finger.

known fact that many *r*s are not pronounced in this dialect.[18] The stereotypical New Yorker will say *Noo Yawk* rather than *New York, cah* rather than *car,* and so on. It is not true that every *r* is eliminated from New York speech. No New Yorker would say *ight* for *right, bing* instead of *bring,* and so forth. Sometimes *r*s are dropped and sometimes they aren't. The name of the game is to determine when they are. One surefire place to lose an *r* in New York speech is in word-final position. *r*s are dropped in words like *beer, far, sore,* and *care.* We can express the deletion process by writing a 0 to the right of the arrow. The members of the input class get changed into nothing (i.e., they are deleted) in a particular context. For simplicity, I dispense with the feature matrix that defines *r* in the rule formalism and write *r.*

(42) *New York* r-*Dropping (Part 1)*
       $r \rightarrow 0 \: / \underline{\hspace{1cm}} \#$

This rule simply says that *r*s are dropped word finally. There is a second context in which New Yorkers regularly drop this segment: before another consonant. Words like *New York, cart, bored, scared,* and *north* are typically pronounced *r*-lessly. I use *C* to represent any consonant. The second context is thus expressed:

(43) *New York* r-*Dropping (Part 2)*
       $r \rightarrow 0 \: / \underline{\hspace{1cm}} C$

Now, we would like to express (42) and (43) as a single process. The input to the rules and their structural changes are identical. Using the curly bracket notation, we arrive at the following formulation:

(44) *New York* r-*Dropping (Combined Form)*
       $r \rightarrow 0 \: / \underline{\hspace{1cm}} \{C, \#\}$

The good news is that it is possible to express the *r*-dropping process as a single phonological rule. The curly brackets have made it possible to collapse two contexts into one. The bad news is that curly brackets can collapse *any* set of contexts into a single disjunctive expression. There is no principled reason why {C,#} forms a more natural context than, say, {[+nasal],[+coronal]}. This latter expression encompasses a set of contexts that are either nasal or coronal. It goes without saying that this expression is totally without interest for any phonological process. In fact, the existence of a set

---

[18]This process is found in a large number of other English dialects, such as the standard or Received Pronunciation (RP) dialect of British English. Readers can mentally replace references to New York English by the *r*-less dialect of their choice.

of expressions within curly brackets is treated as an accident by the theory. Any set of matrices can, in principle, be placed there. But all the good work done by feature theory has been lost! Recall that the natural classes defined by featured matrices imposed a limit on what could be expressed by a phonological rule: what class could undergo a unitary process and what context could trigger a process. With the curly bracket notation system, all that is lost. Recall that in chapter 2 I praised classical generative phonology for the fact that it excluded the possibility of representing the phonologically insignificant set {p,i}. Now, this set can constitute a possible context for some process. Recall also that the avowed objective of generative phonology is to provide a *formal* distinction between possible (or, at least, likely) expressions and those that are impossible. If the theory is working as it should, a possible process should be formally distinguishable from one that is impossible. The curly bracket notation clearly fails to meet this objective; the theory provides no way of explaining why members of the set {C,#} constitute a natural environment for phonological processes, but the members of the set {p,i} do not.

Putting this problem aside for the moment, let us return to the case at hand and suppose the worst: Anything can be a phonological process. It remains the case that the theory treats the disjunctive context _____# or _____C found in rule (44) as an accident. This context has a rating of three (one each for # and C, and one for the curly brackets). It is easy to make up examples with the same rating that are extremely farfetched. Earlier, I gave the example of {[+nasal],[+coronal]}. Our situation would not be so serious if the *r*-dropping context were truly unique, for example, if it were only found in this rule and nowhere else in English or in any other language. We still would have the problem of its relatively low rating, but we might get around that by assigning a very high number of units to the curly brackets. This would be tantamount to saying that the context of the English *r*-dropping rule is very highly marked but possible. English is the language where this rare bird happens to be found. It was just a stroke of luck that we came across this context rather than our *p or i* context. Each is very, very unlikely. This line of argument will not work at all. In fact, the context "word finally or before consonant" is one of the most frequently occurring of all. We find it all over the place. Here are some examples given in informal terms.

(45) *Some Processes Triggered by {_____#,_____C}*

1. In Portuguese, l → w in this context.

2. In Quebec French, palatal nasals (those spelled *gn* in French and pronounced something like *ny* in English *canyon*) become velar (as in English *ng* in *sing*) in this context.

3. German stops and fricatives become voiceless not only in word-final position, as described earlier, but also before certain consonants.

4. In Italian, stressed vowels are lengthened in word-final position or when followed by a single consonant in turn followed by a vowel.

5. In French (any version), a vowel followed by a nasal consonant became a nasal vowel (with the loss of the nasal consonant) in this context. (Cf. *bon, lancer*)

6. In Brazilian Portuguese (Rio de Janeiro and all points north), *s* is pronounced *sh* in this context.

7. In Quebec French, the high vowels *i, ü,* and *u* are laxed (e.g., in the case of *i,* change from the vowel of *heat* to that of *hit*) when followed by a consonant that occurs before this context.

The examples of (45) should dispel any illusions concerning the so-called accidental nature of this context. But things get even worse. Let's look at another example of a process that occurs in this context, one that is known to occur in Quebec French and doubtless exists in other French dialects. The word *tomber* 'to fall' is pronounced [tõbe].[19] This word reflects the process described in (45.5)—the first vowel is nasalized. The final vowel *e* is the infinitive suffix of the first conjugation. When we conjugate this verb in the present indicative, the final suffix is not present. The *b,* which occurs at the end of the verb stem, is now in word-final position. Thus, in a phrase like *je tombe* (the *e* after the *b* is not pronounced) 'I fall', we would expect to hear [tõb]. Indeed, many speakers pronounce this form in exactly this way. In informal speech, however, one frequently hears [tõm] instead. What has happened is that the nasalization of the vowel has affected the final voiced consonant, changing it into the corresponding labial nasal *m*. Similar alternations occur for the other voiced stops. For *demande* 'ask', we get [dmãn] instead of [dmãd]. For *longue* 'long (fem.)', we get [lõŋ][20] instead of [lõg]. What we conclude from all this is that there is an optional process that we can express informally as follows:

(46) *French Stop Nasalization*
A voiced stop becomes nasal in word-final position when preceded by a nasal vowel.

It should come as no surprise by now to learn that the same thing happens when the voiced stop is immediately followed by a consonant. The

---

[19]A nasal vowel is indicated by a superposed tilde

[20]ŋ is the symbol for the velar nasal. This is the sound found in such English words as *sing* and *hanger.*

stem *lõg* is followed by a suffix beginning with a vowel and one beginning with a consonant in the examples below.

(47) a. lõg + ör longueur [lõgör] 'length'
     b. lõg + mã longuement [lõŋmã] 'for a long time'

Once again, we have crossed paths with the context {_____#,_____C}. We fully expect that every time a voiced stop follows a nasal vowel and precedes a word boundary or another consonant, it will be pronounced as a nasal consonant. Consider now the following examples:

(48) combler 'to fill'   encombrer 'to encumber'
     cingler 'to slash'   André   'André'

The verb *combler* is pronounced [kõble]. In this form we have a voiced stop *b*, preceded by a nasal vowel *õ*, followed by a consonant *l*—all the necessary ingredients for the application of our nasalization rule. Yet, the rule does not apply. Application of the rule would yield the pronunciation *[kõmle], which is absolutely impossible. The same may be said for all the other examples of (48). The voiced stop cannot become nasal in any of these forms. In each case, the voiced stop is followed by a liquid, that is *r* or *l*, and thus the forms of (48) represent a true generalization about French. All French words involving liquids behave as those in (48). We must take this fact into account in our formulation of the French nasalization rule, which is now (informally) expressed as follows:

(49) A voiced stop becomes nasal if preceded by a nasal vowel and followed by a consonant *other than a liquid*.

Formally expressed, this rule is a total disaster. The reader can well imagine how many features would be required to formulate all these conditions. The problem worsens when we find the same context with the same additional conditions cropping up again and again. Another example of this type comes to us from English: stress.

English stress is one of the great mysteries of life. Over one hundred pages of SPE are devoted to its analysis. I do not go into any great detail concerning this phenomenon but restrict myself to a group of nouns all ending in *a*.

(50) a. Cánada   b. Aláska
        América   magénta
        Andrómeda   agénda
        Pacífica   Albérta
        Máttawa   Nebráska

In these examples, the acute accent is placed on the stressed syllable. The words in (50a) are all stressed on the antepenultimate (third from the end) syllable. In (50b), all words receive stress on the penultimate (next to the last) syllable. Notice further that in (50a) only one consonant separates the final two vowels. In (50b), two consonants intervene. There is thus a correlation between the position of the stress and the number of consonants that separate the last two vowels of the word. The correlation may be expressed informally as follows:

(51) For words ending in *a*, place the stress on the penultimate vowel if it is followed by two consonants; otherwise, place it on the antepenultimate vowel.[21]

There is a group of words ending in *a* that does not conform to the generalization of (51): *álgebra, vértebra*. These words have antepenultimate stress and yet their penultimate vowel is followed by two consonants. (51) predicts that they should receive stress on their next to last vowel. Further reflection reveals something interesting: In each case, the second of the two consonants is a liquid. Accordingly, we need to revise (51).

(52) For words ending in *a*, place the stress on the penultimate vowel if it is followed by two consonants *the second of which is not a liquid;* otherwise, place it on the antepenultimate vowel.

(52) bears an eerie resemblance to (49). In both cases, we are required to stipulate that a sequence of consonants behaves differently depending on whether or not the second of this cluster is a liquid. Given the theoretical assumptions that we have made so far, this must be treated as an accident. The theory offers no explanation as to why this additional condition is present in both cases.

Let's take stock of the situation. There is a series of rules that require the use of the curly bracket convention. All these rules involve the disjunction of two contexts: _____# and _____C. Furthermore, in a number of cases, the class of consonants mentioned in this context must not include the liquids, *r* and *l*. Our objective is clear: We would like to get rid of the curly brackets, and we would like to explain this mysterious condition involving the liquids. There is a very simple solution to both problems and it involves the syllable. All of the rules mentioned in this section share one important thing: They are sensitive to syllable structure.[22] Up to this point, the theory

---

[21]This generalization is not without exceptions: *Montána, banána*, etc.

[22]We are now about to enter into a detailed discussion of the role of syllable structure in phonological processes. Like all other phonological objects, syllables are cognitive rather than

has made no mention of syllable structure. The problems now confronting us are the result of this theoretical gap.

Remember the r-dropping context in New York English. If we use syllable structure, it becomes trivial to express this process.

(53) *New York r-Dropping (Syllable Version)*
   r → 0 in syllable-final position

r is lost at the end of syllables. To see how, let's consider some examples.

(54) a. caɾ   b. caɾ$ton   c. pu$trid
     beeɾ   im$poɾ$tant   ee$rie
     teaɾ   poɾ$trait   se$rene
     touɾ   faɾ$meɾ   re$frain

In the examples of (54), ɾ indicates an r that is dropped in New York speech. $ represents a syllable boundary—the division between two syllables. The words in (54a) all end in r. We assume that a syllable boundary corresponds to the word boundary in these cases. All the rs in (54a) are thus in syllable- (and word-) final position. According to (53) they should be dropped, and so they are. The words in (54b) are polysyllabic, with $ marking the syllable divisions. In each case, r is found just before a syllable boundary. Because it is in syllable-final position, it satisfies the context of (53). Once again, (53) correctly predicts the results. In contrast, the rs of (54c) do not occur before a syllable boundary. Deleting any of them is completely out of the question. No one can say eeɾie for eerie or refɾain for refrain. Thus, allowing syllable structure in the expression of phonological contexts results in both a formal and a conceptual simplification. To complete the story of New York r-dropping, a word should be said about forms like maɾk, poɾt, absoɾb. In these cases, each word appears to be monosyllabic. If this were the case, no syllable boundary would immediately follow the deleted r. Rather, the syllable boundary would correspond to the word boundary and follow the final consonant. If we accepted this superficial analysis, we would have to complicate the context of this rule accordingly. I will not go into the details here, but there is good evidence to suppose that a syllable boundary does follow the r in forms like mark. The correct representation would be marˢk. Technically speaking, the $ represents the boundary between a rime and the following constituent in the theory of the syllable sketched out in the begin-

_____

physical. This is to say that one will not find direct correlates of their presence in the acoustic signal. There are a myriad of indirect indicators of syllable structure in the acoustic signal. The processes soon to be discussed are but a tiny fragment of these indicators.

ning of this chapter. In the context given in (55), one merely needs to change the word *syllable* to *rime* and everything is taken care of.

Let's turn now to the mysterious behavior of liquids. The first case involved the nasalization of French voiced stops. Using the syllable, we can now dispense with the curly brackets and at the same time solve the problem of the liquids. Here is the formulation of the rule using syllable structure.

(55)   A voiced stop becomes nasal if it is preceded by a nasal vowel *in the same syllable*.

Let us apply this new formulation to the original examples repeated in (56) for convenience.

(56) a.   tõb   tombe   b.   tõ$be   tomber
            dmãd   demande   dmã$de   demander
            lõg   longue   lõ$gör   longueur

      c.   kõ$ble   combler   d.   lõg$mã   longuement
            ã$dre   André
            sẽ$gle   cingler

In (56a), each word ends in a single voiced stop. This stop is in the same syllable as the nasal vowel (the only syllable of the word) and thus undergoes nasalization, yielding [tõm], [dmãn], and [lõŋ], respectively. The forms of (56b) are bisyllabic. Crucially, the syllable boundary falls between the nasal vowel and the following voiced stop. This latter segment forms the onset of the following syllable, whose nucleus is the initial vowel of the suffix (-*e* or -*ör*). I have not given any arguments for this syllabification. These cases are quite uncontroversial and correspond to the way native speakers of French break up words into syllables. In general, a single consonant always combines with a following vowel in the same syllable unless there is a major constituent boundary (morpheme, word, or phrase) that separates them. English compound boundaries are strong enough to prevent syllabifying a final consonant with a following vowel. Compare the forms *night owl* versus *dry towel*. There is a clear difference in syllabification of these two forms. In the first case, the final *t* of *night* does not form a unit with the initial vowel of *owl*. A compound boundary separates them. In the second case, the initial *t* and the following *ow* are in the same word and the same syllable. In French, a stem-final consonant will be invariably syllabified with a suffix-initial vowel. This is what happens to the forms of (56b), and this is what explains the position of the syllable boundary. The reader should not expect syllable boundaries to be always so obvious.[23] In this case, it works out that way.

The forms of (56c) contain internal sequences of voiced stop plus liquid. These sequences are grouped together in a single constituent: a branching onset. As such as they are not in the same syllable as the nasal vowel, and the voiced stop is thus not subject to the rule of nasalization. Once more, the syllabification of (56c) corresponds to the intuitions of native speakers. Further evidence that the syllable boundaries in (56c) are indeed correctly placed exists but will not be discussed here.

Incorporation of syllable structure into phonological representations provides us with a way to distinguish two types of consonant clusters (sequences of consonants): *tautosyllabic clusters,* contained within a single syllabic constituent (namely, the onset), and *heterosyllabic clusters,* where a syllable boundary falls between members of the cluster. In general, the onset constituent (the tautosyllabic case) consists of a stop or fricative followed by a liquid. The fact that liquids have the special status of being permitted as the second member of an onset accounts for their popping up time and time again in the contexts of syllable-sensitive phonological processes. Most sequences of consonants are not found in the same syllable (the heterosyllabic cases). The first member of the sequence normally is grouped together with the preceding vowel. This is what gives the impression that a consonant followed by another consonant or by a word boundary constitutes a legitimate context for a phonological rule. But all this is an illusion. What is really important here is the location of the syllable boundaries. They are what trigger the application of these processes. Thus, when the sequence of consonants consists of a stop plus a liquid, things start to change. It is precisely this sequence that can constitute the onset of a syllable. If the stop is in the onset of the *following* syllable, it cannot form part of the preceding syllable. Specifically, it is not in the same syllable as the preceding vowel. In French, the spreading of nasalization to a following voiced stop occurs only within a syllable and not across a syllable boundary. Stop plus liquid sequences are together the onset of the following syllable, therefore no stop followed by a liquid can undergo this nasalization. This all follows from a universal theory of syllable structure along the lines of that sketched out in this chapter. For French stop nasalization, all that need be said is that it applies within the syllable. The details fall out from general theoretical considerations.

The same reasoning can be applied to the case of English stress. We can

---

[23]For example, there is good reason to believe that *s* and *t* are not in the same syllable in a word like *stop*.

reformulate the stress rule for words ending in *a* using information about syllable structure. The new version of this rule follows:

(57) For words ending in *a*, stress the penultimate syllable if it is closed (i.e., if it ends in a consonant); otherwise, stress the antepenultimate syllable.

In light of (57), consider the following forms:

(58) a. Cánada   b. A$lás$ka   c. álgebra

In (58a), the penultimate syllable *na* ends in a vowel and therefore is an open syllable. Stress is accordingly placed on the antepenultimate syllable, yielding the desired result. In (58b), there is a syllable break between the *s* and the *k*,[24] thus the penultimate syllable is *las,* a closed syllable. The rule says that in this case the next to last syllable should be stressed, and so it is. Finally, we come to the case of *algebra*. Here, the consonant cluster separating the last two vowels is *br,* a stop plus liquid sequence. This cluster is analyzed as a branching onset; specifically, it begins the final syllable. Therefore, the penultimate syllable is open; it ends in a vowel. It cannot be stressed. The stress is predictably on the antepenultimate syllable.

The moral of all this is that inclusion of syllable structure allows us to get rid of the most common use of the dreaded curly brackets. It explains what would otherwise be a completely mysterious ancillary condition involving liquids. We return to a phonological theory that has a good deal more predictive power concerning what is and what is not a phonological process. This line of argument has won over the vast majority of phonologists,[25] and one finds reference to syllable structure in most modern analyses. The relevance of syllable structure goes beyond theoretical considerations. In the next chapter I discuss its practical applications.

The decision to incorporate syllable structure into phonological representations constituted a significant departure from the *linear* approach that characterizes SPE. Classical generative phonology postulated a single level of phonological structure. Representations were two dimensional: Along the horizontal axis, one placed the feature matrices representing individual segments. Each phonological feature had its assigned place along the ver-

---

[24]This is one case where speakers' intuitions are not too reliable. There is unmistakable evidence that *s* + *consonant* sequences are not tautosyllabic in any language.

[25]That is, arguments for the existence of a level of syllable structure relevant to the expression of phonological processes. There is still a good deal of debate concerning the exact nature of syllable structure.

tical axis. To this arrangement one must add an additional level of structure: that of the syllable. We see in the next sections that this departure from a strictly linear type of representation is not at all limited to the syllable.

Tones and Autosegmental Phonology

We have just seen how considerations involving syllable structure led phonologists to depart from the SPE-type representations. During this same period, research on tonal systems were leading to the same conclusion: Phonological representations are not linear. To give the reader an appreciation of the impact of this work and its consequences for phonological theory, I offer an explanation of what tones are.

When we speak English we imagine that the identification of individual words is made based exclusively on the sequence of consonants and vowels. The word *boy* is the sequence *b, o, y* or the equivalent expressed as feature matrices. By and large, this is generally true, although there are a few pairs of words in English that are distinct and have distinct pronunciations but whose differences are not defined in terms of phonological segments. Consider the following pairs:

(59) a. récord   b. recórd
          cónvert   convért
          pérfect   perféct
          cómpress   compréss

What distinguishes the pairs in (59) is not so much differences in segmental structure (the consonants and vowels), but rather the position of the stress (indicated again by an acute accent). The words of (59a), nouns and adjectives, have stress on their initial syllable. The forms of (59b), all verbs, have final stress. It is true that the vowel quality is affected by whether or not it is stressed. That is, the initial vowel of *récord* is not quite identical to that of *recórd* (most people say *ruhcórd* rather than *rehcórd*). This difference is tributary to the stress, however. Let us assume then that, in terms of segments, these pairs have the same representations. What distinguishes them is the position of the stress. Phenomena such as stress that do not directly involve individual segments are called *prosodic phenomena*. Prosodic phenomena are rather marginal in English, at least at the level of words. It is true that stress distinguishes certain words such as those listed in (59), but there are other differences as well. In the case of English, verbs have a different stress pattern than nouns and adjectives. Each pair involves such a change of category. Ultimately, the difference in stress can be ascribed to the difference in grammatical category.

Tone languages[26] (i.e., languages that have tone) are like the English stress example taken to an extreme. Rather than being limited to a handful of examples, the vocabulary of a tone language is full of instances where words are distinguished solely on the basis of a prosodic property. In English, stress is manifested by a variety of phonetic factors: A stressed vowel is typically longer, produced with greater intensity and at a higher fundamental frequency (higher pitched). Tone languages employ fundamental frequency (F_0) as the phonetic manifestation of tone. What this means is that in tone languages, words may be distinguished solely on the basis of the fundamental frequency of their vowels.

To illustrate this I take examples from Vata, a language spoken in the Ivory Coast. Let's begin with the sequence *la*. There is nothing exotic in this. The sequence consists of an *l* very much like the *l* in English. It is followed by the vowel *a* (as in English *father*). Together, they form a syllable pretty much like the English pronunciation of the note *la*. In Vata, however, the story does not stop there. If *la* is pronounced with a relatively high fundamental frequency, it means 'to call'. If it is pronounced with a lower frequency, it means 'to carry'. To proceed with this discussion I need to introduce some conventions for writing these tones. I provide symbols for four different levels of tone because this is the number of distinctions that Vata manifests.

(60)   *Tonal Transcriptions* (a = *Any Vowel*)

High Tone	á
Mid–High Tone	a̍
Mid Tone	a
Low Tone	à

The highest tone (i.e., with the highest fundamental frequency) is indicated with an acute accent on the vowel that bears it. The next tone down is the mid–high tone, indicated with a vertical accent. Vowels with a mid tone have no accent. Finally, the low tone is marked with a grave accent. Now, let's look at some Vata forms.

(61)   a̍ lá   'you (pl.) call'   a̍ là   'you (pl.) carry'
       à lá̍   'we call'   à la   'we carry'
                                    à là   'we carried'

---

[26]Tone languages are found all over the world. The continents of Asia and Africa are well represented by tone languages. They are also found in reasonable numbers in the indigenous languages of North and South America.

In (61), we see that *la* can appear with all four tones. We have *lá* meaning 'call' preceded by the pronoun *á* 'you (pl.)', *lá*, meaning 'call' following the pronoun *à* 'we' or meaning 'carry' after the pronoun *á*, *la* meaning 'carry' after the pronoun *à*, and *là* meaning 'carried' after the pronoun *à*. All this may seem horribly complicated but it is really quite simple. What we have here are two verb stems: one meaning 'call' and the other meaning 'carry'. These verbs stems have identical segmental forms: *la*. They are distinguished by their tone. Thus, tone forms part of a lexical representation of a word in the same sense that consonants and vowels do.[27] To have a complete picture of the representation of the verb *call* we not only need to indicate that it consists of *l* followed by *a* but also that it has a particular tone. Things seem complicated because the forms meaning 'call' do not always have the same tone. But this is just another phonological phenomenon, this time involving tone. Let's see how such phenomena may be described in a linear framework.

We can follow the established analytical procedure and choose one tone as the starting point and derive all the other manifestations via phonological rules. Let's say that the underlying (i.e., lexical) tone for the verb *call* is mid high. It doesn't matter for the moment how we come to this conclusion. We now have a complete representation for the verb *call: lá* (of course, the segments would be represented as feature matrices in a completely formal rendition), and everything becomes much easier. No work is required to derive *à lá* 'we call'. The verb manifests its lexical tone; nothing has changed. We do need a story for the second person plural form *á* lá, we would expect *á* lá. Here, the verb appears with a high tone rather than its lexical mid-high tone. The only phonological difference between the two forms of the conjugation is the tone of the pronoun. In one case, it is low and nothing happens; in the other case, it is mid high and the tone of the verb goes up a notch to a high tone. All we need to do is to write a rule. The rule could be expressed informally as follows:

(62) A mid-high tone becomes high when preceded by another mid-high tone.

This rule can be expressed just like any purely segmental process in an SPE format. We can choose two appropriate features to distinguish the four

---

[27]In tone languages with a written tradition such as Vietnamese, tones are part of the spelling of a given word. Vietnamese uses accents placed above vowels to indicate tones in the written forms.

tones, say [higher] and [peripheral]. This gives us the following matrices for the four tones in question:

(63) *Feature Representations of Tone*

	Higher	*Peripheral*
High	+	+
Mid-High	+	−
Mid	−	−
Low	−	+

The feature [peripheral] divides the tonal scale in half. [+peripheral] indicates the tones at the two extremes of the scale. [−peripheral] refers to the two tones in the middle of the scale. Within each division the higher of the two tones is [+higher] and the lowest tone is [−higher]. Whether these are the best features on which to base tonal distinctions is not at issue here. I only wish to show that tonal phenomena are amenable to exactly the same kind of analysis and representation as any other phonological feature. We can now formalize rule (62) using these features.

(64) [+higher] → [+peripheral] / [+higher]#C_____

That is, a high or mid-high tone will become high when preceded by another high or mid-high tone. This rule is more general than the data presented earlier. It will serve our purposes here.

The alternations involving the verb *carry* are similar in nature to those we have already discussed. We need to choose a lexical tone for this verb and formulate a rule to derive cases where the phonetic form departs from the underlying representation. This verb occurs with three different tones in our examples: a mid-high tone following a pronoun with a mid-high tone, a mid tone following a pronoun with a low tone, and a low tone in the form translated by a past tense.[28] This latter form cannot be a manifestation of a phonological process because we find it in an identical context to that in which a mid tone occurs: *à la* (mid tone) 'we carry', *à là* (low tone) 'we carried'. In both cases, the verb is preceded by a pronoun with a low tone. Limiting ourselves to the purely phonological phenomenon, we find *lá* (mid-high tone) following a mid-high tone and *la* (mid tone) following a low tone. Let's choose the mid tone as the lexical tone of the verb *to carry*. Once more, the form occurring after the low toned pronoun poses no problem. We start with a verb having a mid tone and that's what we wind

---

[28]This is in fact a perfective aspect form, indicating that the action in question has been completed. It is usually translated by a past tense in English.

up with: *à la*. To account for the mid-high tone in *á lá*, we need to say something like the following:

(65) A mid tone becomes mid-high when preceded by another mid-high tone.

Rule (65) bears a striking resemblance to (62). There is certainly a way of combining them to produce a single rule encompassing both processes. I will not pursue this because, as we shall soon see, the SPE-type treatment of tonal phenomena is rejected by almost all phonologists today. In any event, we can now account for all but the final form of the data in (60). Here are the derivations:

(66)	à lá	à la	á lá	á la
Rule (64)	—	—	á lá	—
Rule (65)	—	—	—	á lá
Output	à lá	à la	á lá	á lá

If we do not combine rules (64) and (65), it is important that rule (64) apply before rule (65) in the derivations. Rule (65) will raise a mid tone to a mid-high tone following another mid-high tone. We have produced a sequence of a mid-high pronoun followed by a verb with a mid-high tone. But this is exactly the input to rule (64) that raises a mid-high tone to high following another mid-high tone. Reversing the order of (64) and (65) would produce the incorrect result *[á lá] meaning 'you (pl.) carry'. To avoid this problem, either we combine the two processes or we stipulate (as we did in (66) that rule (64) must apply before rule (65).

This brings us to the form *à là* (low tones) 'we carried'. I have already shown that the appearance of a low tone on the verb *to carry* cannot be due to purely phonological causes. If this were the case, we could not account for the fact that this same verb appears with a mid tone after the same pronoun in the form *à la* 'we carry.' It is clear that the change in tone is what indicates the change in aspect (roughly, the change in tense). In this sense, Vata resembles English, where a change in category (verb to noun or adjective) can be accompanied by a change in stress. Thus, we need to include grammatical information in the context of a rule that will change a mid tone to a low tone.

(67) A mid tone becomes low in the perfective aspect.

This will produce the form *à là*, which is what we want.

The discussion of Vata served as an introduction (a very brief one) to tonal phenomena. I want to emphasize that such processes received exactly the same treatment as the more familiar segmental processes in linear phonology. In certain languages, called *tone languages,* tonal features formed a part of the lexical representation of morphemes. Under this approach phonological rules could manipulate these features, just as they could manipulate any of the other features associated with phonological segments. Tone played no special role in linear phonology. The only evidence of its existence in a language was the inclusion of those features specific to it in the matrices of vowels. Thus, the phonological representations of tone languages were formally identical to the representations of nontone languages.

Let me end this introduction by dispelling one misconception concerning tone languages. Often one hears the remark, "Oh, I could never speak a tone language [say, Chinese]. I can't carry a tune." Tonal distinctions are always relative, never absolute. All that is required is to detect that one tone is higher/lower/equal with respect to another. No tone language exists where a high tone is, say, exactly a minor third above a mid tone. The base line of a tonal system varies according to the individual and may even vary in various pronunciations of the same individual. A low tone is not defined as an F_0 of 400 Hz. The intervals between tones are also not fixed on an absolute scale. In a four-tone system such as that of Vata, all we need to know is that the relative pitches of each of the tones respects the tonal scale. In a given domain (a phrase), a high tone should be produced at a higher pitch than a mid-high tone and so on.[29] Every normal human being has the ability to distinguish relative pitch levels. Every normal human being can learn a tone language (as a native language) with equal facility.

We have seen that it is possible to describe tonal phenomena using the formalism of classical generative phonology. The fact remains that today virtually no phonologist believes that the tonal analysis presented for Vata is anything more than utter nonsense. The linear approach to phonology—representations involving sequences of feature matrices—is no longer taken seriously. It is precisely the study of tonal phenomena that was a major cause for abandoning the SPE model. Let's look at some of the reasons for this.

John Goldsmith (1976), following earlier work done by Edwin Williams (1976) and Will Leben (1973), presented a series of arguments showing that the linear model of SPE was inappropriate for the expression of tonal phenomena. I summarize his three principle arguments here.

---

[29]I am oversimplifying here. A fascinating question is whether a speaker of a tone language can recognize, say, a high tone with no other context to fix the base line. Suppose a Vata speaker simply said, "Lá" 'call!'. Would other speakers of the language recognize this form for what it is? I believe this is the case. This implies that tonal levels do have some absolute measure that is necessarily distinct from mere fundamental frequency. My feeling is that this involves tension of the vocal cords. A high tone is produced when vocal cords are tightened

In my examples from Vata, I discussed four different tones. These tones have one property in common: There is no significant shift of frequency in the course of their pronunciation. That is, they finish at more or less the same frequency at which they start. These types of tones are called *level tones*. There is another type of tone, common to most tonal systems, where a significant shift in pitch takes place between the beginning and the end of its production. Thus, in addition to the level tones we can find *rising tones* (the frequency goes up) and *falling tones*. These are called *contour tones*. Early on in the analysis of tonal systems, it was unclear how contour tones should be represented. Strict adherence to the linear model dictated the use of features such as [rising] or [falling]. Other phonologists proposed a less orthodox device, namely the use of complex matrices. Complex matrices themselves contained submatrices. A rising tone could thus be represented by a matrix that included, in addition to the appropriate vowel features, a complex expression of the form [[−higher][+higher]]. This is something like chopping a segment in half and assigning [−higher] to the first half and [+higher] to the second. All other features remained constant throughout the production of the segment. While there were certain advantages to this complex matrix approach, it also increased the expressive power of the theory to a significant degree. If one could divide a segment in half and assign differing values of [higher] to each half, why couldn't one do the same thing with any other feature? For example, it should be equally likely to find complex matrices where the dividing feature is [coronal]. The problem is that no known segment was partially coronal and partially non-coronal. By the early 1970s, phonologists were generally dissatisfied with tonal analyses.

Goldsmith's first argument involved contour tones. His proposition was that contour tones are sequences of level tones: A rising tone was a sequence of a low tone followed by a high tone; a falling tone was a sequence of a high tone followed by a low tone. This position is similar in spirit to the complex matrix approach, but its formal implementation carried us far away from the linear model of classical generative phonology. Let's first look at Goldsmith's arguments for a compositional analysis (i.e., an analysis into sequences of level tones) of contour tones. Goldsmith presented some data from a dialect of Igbo, a language spoken in Nigeria. This example concerns a tonal effect that occurs on the final syllable of certain nouns, but not pronouns. The first examples show some pronominal forms followed by a low toned verb (Goldsmith, 1976, p. 43).[30]

(just like a guitar string) beyond a certain neutral position. I speculate that this glottal tensing is perceptible and serves as a cue for a high tone, at least in the simplest cases.

[30]Igbo lax vowels are italicized. As before, an acute accent indicates a high tone; and a grave accent, a low tone.

(68) ó   cì   àkhwá   'he was carrying some eggs'
      he   carry   eggs

      ó   zà   úlò   'he must sweep the house'
      he   sweep house

Note the high tone on the pronoun *ó* 'he'. Nouns may end in a high tone or a low tone. What follows are examples of nouns with final low tone (Goldsmith, 1976, p. 44):

(69) ézà cì   àkhwá   'the chief was carrying eggs'
      chief carry eggs

      ùwà cì   àkhwá   'Uwa was carrying eggs'

Nothing much is happening here. The tone on the nouns *ézà* and *ùwà* remain unchanged before the verb *cì*. The action begins when a noun ends in a high tone. Goldsmith (1976, p. 44) provides two examples.

(70) ékwê cì àkhwá   'Ekwe was carrying eggs'
      àdhâ cì àkhwá   'Adha was carrying eggs'

The circumflex accent on the vowels indicates a falling tone. In isolation the two names, *ékwé* and *àdhá,* end in high tones. What we need to say is that a noun-final high tone becomes a falling tone when followed by a low tone, which sounds pretty arbitrary. Why should a high tone become a falling tone before a low tone? It is not immediately obvious why this process should be more natural than, say, one that changes a low tone into a falling tone before another low tone. In fact, the former process—the one that underlies the examples in (70)—is commonplace, whereas the latter process has never been attested. Yet, there seems to be no formal difference between the two tonal processes. This illusion disappears if we think of a falling tone, the one occurring on the final syllable of the subject nouns in (70), as a sequence of a high tone followed by a low tone. To sharpen this idea, I extract the tonal pattern from the first sentence in (70). I indicate a high tone with *H* and a low tone with *L*. The presumed input to the first sentence in (70) is *ékwé cì àkhwá* (recall that ékwé is pronounced with two high tones in isolation). The initial tonal melody is thus, H H # L # L H (the sharp sign # indicates a word boundary). The end result that appears in (70) is H HL # L # L H. (I have written the contour falling tone as HL.) The only difference between these two melodies is that an additional low tone has attached itself to the noun final high tone. The source of this low tone is now obvious; it must come from the low tone that immediately follows, that is, the low tone on the verb *cì*. This tonal phenomenon falls under the general heading of an assimilation process. The utilization of tonal melodies and the analysis of contour tones as sequences of level tones explain the vast difference between this phenomenon and the putative process whereby a low tone becomes a falling tone before another low tone. Expressing this in melodic forms gives the following:

(71) ... L # L ... → ... HL # L

In (71), a high tone mysteriously arises from nowhere to form a falling tone. There is no apparent source for this high tone and no reason why it should attach itself to a low tone followed by another low tone. This process is indeed completely arbitrary. If it is true that (71) is impossible, it would be very nice to formulate a theory that would permit us to express the Igbo phenomenon while rendering something like (71) inexpressible. This is one of the virtues of *autosegmental phonology*. Goldsmith proposed a departure from a strictly linear representation. Tones would be represented on one level, and segments on another.[31] The two levels would be joined by *association lines*. A lexical representation would consist of an ordered list of segments and an ordered list of tones. By convention, the tones are associated to the appropriate segments (usually vowels) in a one-to-one fashion going from left to right. Goldsmith also proposed the following well-formedness convention for autosegmental representations:

(72) Association lines may not cross.

We can now apply this to the Igbo example. The representation of *ékwê cì àkhwá* would be:

(73) Tone Level   H H # L   L H
     Segmental Level   ekwe # ci # akhwa

We now associate the tones to the segments following the recipe given in (73).

(74) H H   # L # L   H
     | | | | |
     ekwe # ci # akhwa

A high tone is simply the unit H on the tonal level lined up with a vowel on the segmental level via an association line.

---

[31]As Goldsmith points out, the germ of this idea date back to the 1940s. Firth (1948) proposed a division of this kind in phonological representations. At approximately the same time, Harris (1944) expressed similar ideas.

Obviously, we are not getting full mileage out of this formalism if we stick to a one-to-one relation between tone and segments. The fun starts when we deal with many-to-one or one-to-many relations between these two levels. We see this when we express the formation of contour tones in Igbo. Recall that this occurs when a final high tone of a noun is followed by a verb with a low tone. The form in (74) satisfies this condition. So what happens next? It's all quite simple. We make one stipulation: The low tone on the verb spreads to its left, making a second linkage with the final vowel of the noun.

(75)   H H   L L   H
       | |╱| | |
       ekwe ci akhwa

The final vowel of *ékwê* has two tones associated with it: the high tone, which forms part of its lexical representation, followed by a low tone, which has spread from its right. Here, we have two units on the tonal level associated with a single segment. This is now the exact definition of a contour tone.

Recall that in the examples of (69) nouns ending in a low tone underwent no change. Can this be explained by autosegmental theory? Yes, indeed! Let's look at the sentence *ùwà à àkhwá*. Its autosegmental representation is as follows:

(76)   L L   L L   H
       | | | | |
       uwa ci akhwa

Keeping things simple, let's also suppose that the Igbo spreading rule applies to any preceding tone (excluding pronouns) and not just to high toned forms: A low tone on a verb spreads to the final syllable of a preceding noun. This yields (77).

(77)   L L   L L   H
       | |╱| | |
       uwa ci akhwa

The final vowel of *ùwà* is associated with two low tones: its lexical low tone and the low tone that spread over from the verb. It is quite natural to interpret a vowel associated with two low tones as being exactly the same as a vowel with a single low tone. The image is a bit like shutting down a computer by turning off the switch or pulling out the plug. Performing either act, or both in either order, has, by and large, the same effect. The screen of the monitor does not get any blanker if one pulls out the plug after having shut off the machine. Adding a low tone to a vowel that already has a low tone does not make the tone any lower. The prediction is that a noun ending with a low tone should not change at all if it is followed by a verb with a low tone. This is exactly correct.

Autosegmental phonology also gives us a way of understanding the Vata data presented previously. These forms are repeated in (78).

(78) á lá 'you (pl.) call'   á là 'you (pl.) carry'
      à lǎ 'we call'   à la 'we carry'
                               à là 'we carried'

What interests us here is the perfective form *à là* 'we carried'. As I have indicated, the low tone on the verb cannot be derived from purely phonological sources. It must reflect, at least in part, the formal mark of the perfective aspect. To pursue this line of inquiry, let me give the perfective forms of both verbs along with their present tense (in reality their imperfective) forms.

(79) *Imperfective*   lǎ 'to call'   la 'to carry'
      Perfective   à lǎ 'to call'   à la 'we carry'
                        à lǎ 'we called'   à là 'we carried'

Let's assume that the perfective form consists of the imperfective form plus something else. The starting point is then the first line of (79), where we see the lexical representations of the imperfective forms for both verbs. Our objective is to derive the perfective forms. As we have already seen, the perfective form of *la* 'to carry' involves placing a low tone on the verb. It is natural to assume that the low tone marks the perfective aspect. We can consider that this low tone is a suffix, just as -*ed* is a suffix in English, as in *walked*. In tone languages, prefixes and suffixes may consist of tones, with no associated segmental material. What this means is that the recipe for forming a perfective form in Vata is as follows:

(80) *Vata Perfective Forms*
      Add a low tone to the imperfective form. If T is some tone and V is some vowel then

$$\begin{array}{c} T \\ | \\ V \end{array} = \text{Imperfective} \qquad \begin{array}{cc} T & L \\ | & \\ V & \end{array} = \text{Perfective}$$

Suppose certain verbs in Vata have no lexical tone. What would be the effect of adding a low toned suffix to them? Given the principles of autosegmental theory, we would expect the following:

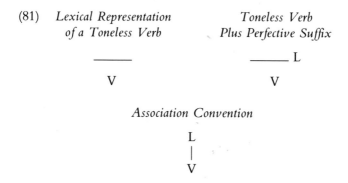

(81) *Lexical Representation*   *Toneless Verb*
      of a Toneless Verb   *Plus Perfective Suffix*

     ——————   —————— L

        V   V

Association Convention

L
|
V

Crucially, the final result of this operation is a verb with a low tone—exactly the perfective form of *à là*.

Let us now consider another situation. The description in (81) is all well and good as long as there is a tonal suffix around to associate with the verb. What about the imperfective form? What tone is produced when this form occurs alone? The answer is that it is pronounced with a mid tone; a tone that is neither high nor low. Suppose we consider the absence of tone to correspond to what has been traditionally called a mid tone. What this implies is that any vowel that winds up at the end of a derivation with no tonal association is produced with a mid tone.[32] Thus, the representation of the imperfective form of *la* is simply that: *la* with no lexical tone. A toneless vowel is lower than a high tone and higher than a low tone. It has been traditionally called a mid tone. In the perfective form, we add a low tone suffix. Then we apply the tonal association conventions. We link each tone to each vowel going from left to right. The verb has one vowel, *a* and one tone *L*. We link *L* to *a* and this gives us (82).

(82)   L
                        |

                      la

---

[32]Here, I depart from the original proposals found in Goldsmith (1976). Pulleyblank (1983) presented the idea of an unmarked or default tone. The presentation here differs in some significant ways from Pulleyblank's theory. I do not enter into the details of this debate here. My purpose is to explore the formal possibilities of autosegmental representations.

(82) is the correct representation of the perfective form. Let's take the other verb, *lá* 'to call'. This is not a toneless verb; it has a lexical mid-high tone (MH).[33] Its representation in the perfective aspect is shown in (83).

(83) MH   L
     |
    la

Notice that in (83) there are more tones (two) than vowels (one). In such a case, autosegmental theory instructs us to associate the residual tone with the vowel to its left. This is shown in (84).

(84) MH   L
    la

The vowel of the verb now has two tones associated with it: the lexical mid-high tone and the low tone marking the perfective suffix. This should result in a contour tone that begins at the mid-high level and falls to the low level. This is precisely the perfective form of this verb. It corresponds to what I have transcribed *lâ*. Once again, it is clear that a contour tone is composed of a sequence of level tones. The autosegmental representation of tones allows us to capture the various aspects of tonal behavior in an insightful manner.

The second argument presented by Goldsmith for a separate level of tonal representation involves the notion of stability. If tones and segments indeed march to two different drummers, then we can expect to observe processes that affect the segmental level while leaving the tonal level intact. The association conventions will tell us where to place the tones once the segmental changes have occurred. A typical situation of this kind is when a vowel is deleted. More often than not, its tone remains to reassociate to some other available vowel. In Lomongo, another African language, certain consonants are deleted phrase internally. This deletion creates a sequence of two vowels, the first of which is deleted. It is this latter process that interests us. We can now observe the behavior of a tone once its vowel is deleted out from under it. Consider the following example (Goldsmith [1976, p. 58] taken from Lovins, 1971):

(85) bàlóngó (b)ǎkáé → bàlóngākáé 'his book'

---

[33]Remember that a mid-high tone, its name and symbol notwithstanding, is a *single* level tone and not a sequence of a mid tone followed by a high tone.

The initial syllable of the word *bǎkáé* 'book' has a rising tone, represented as *ǎ*. At the end of the derivation, this vowel winds up with a contour tone that first falls (= H L) and then rises (= L H). In other words, this syllable carries three tones! A vowel with three tones is rather rare but not unheard of (no pun intended). Autosegmental theory allows us to derive this result in a straightforward manner. We pick up the derivation after the deletion of the initial *b* of the word *book*.

(86)   L H   H   L   H HH
    | | | ∨ | |
    bal ongo   a   k   a e

Next, the first vowel of the sequence *o a* is deleted.[34] This gives us (87).

(87)   L H   H   L   H HH
    | | ∨ | |
    bal ong   a   k   a e

The tone that was formerly linked to *o* is now set free. It will seek out a vowel on which to dock. There are two possibilities: It could dock to the left, joining the high tone already linked to the vowel *o,* or it could dock to the right, joining the two tones that are linked to the vowel *a.* The theory provides no a priori answer as to the direction of docking in such cases. Both solutions are possible. In Lomongo, it turns out that the liberated tone docks to the right, forming a double contour tone.

(88)   L H   H   L   H HH
    | | ∨∕ | |
    bal ong   a   k   a e

Once more, the autosegmental representation of tone allows us to provide a principled account of these data. Comparing the tonal tier of (86), (87), and (88) shows that no tone change has taken place on this level. What happens on the segmental tier leaves the tonal tier unaffected. The only tonal change involves reassociating the tone cut loose by the loss of a vowel with one of the remaining vowels. All this points to two separate levels of representation: a tonal tier and a segmental tier.

To this point, we have seen cases where the number of tones exceeds the number of vowels with which they can associate. This normally leads to the formation of contour tones, resulting from a multiple association of several

---

[34]It is not clear why the first vowel of the sequence *áé* is not also deleted.

(different) tones to one vowel. Recall that the basic tenet of autosegmental phonology is the autonomy of the tonal tier with respect to the segmental tier. If this view is correct, not only do we expect to find the kinds of examples already shown—cases where the number of tones exceeds the number of vowels—but also situations where the number of vowels exceeds the number of tones. Let us see what happens when there are not enough tones to go around.

The association conventions provide the answer. We link up tones and vowels going from left to right. If more vowels remain after linking the last tone, this tone spreads to all the remaining vowels. We can return to Vata to find an example of this sort. If we add a toneless suffix to a stem carrying a lexical tone, we have a situation where the vowels outnumber the tones. We expect that the final lexical tone will spread to the remaining toneless syllables. In Vata, the instrumental/locative suffix -le has no lexical tone. It can be freely added to many verbs. Let's look at two in particular: klá 'to chop down' and kla 'to grab'. The relevant forms follow:

(89)   klá   'to chop down'   kla   'to grab'
  Imperfective klá-lé   'chops down with'   kla-le 'grabs with'
  Perfective   klá-lè   'chopped down with' klà-lè 'grabbed
                                                       with'

In the imperfective forms, the tone on the suffix -le is identical to the preceding tone, as predicted. In the perfective forms, the suffix invariably bears a low tone. All these data fall out automatically if one assumes that -le has no lexical tone.

(90) *Imperfective*

MH   MH
 | →   ⟍
kla = le kla = le = [klálé]   klla = le = [klale]

Perfective

MH L   MH L   L   L
 | → | | → ⟍
kla-le   kla-l e   kla-le   kl a-le

Consider first the imperfective form of klá-lè. There is one tone, the MH tone on the first syllable, and two vowels. The mid-high tone spreads to the suffix vowel yielding a form with a mid-high tone on each of the two syllables. What autosegmental theory tells us is that these are not two separate entities but rather a single tone associated with two distinct vowels.

This is simply the mirror image of a contour tone, where we had two distinct tones linked to a single vowel. The imperfective form *kla-le* is quite simple. There is literally nothing to say. No tones are present on either vowel. Nothing can spread. A toneless vowel has what we have called a mid tone. Both syllables of this form should be realized with a mid tone, and so they are.

Recall that the perfective forms include a low tone suffix. We have seen that vowels can occur without tone. Here is a case of a tone without a vowel. With the addition of this suffix, there is an equal number of tones and vowels. As one expects, the low tone links to the toneless suffix and we get *klá-lè*. The case of the toneless verb *kla* is more interesting. The suffix tone L links to the leftmost available vowel (i.e., a vowel without a tone). In this case, the stem vowel has no tone and so the low tone associates with it. There remains the suffix vowel, which also has no tone. Following the conventions, the low tone spreads to it, yielding a form with a low tone on each syllable. Once again, this is but a multiple manifestation of a single object: the low tone of the perfective suffix. The logical possibilities offered to us by autosegmental representations (the many-to-one associations in both directions) are thus fully attested in tonal systems.

The final piece of evidence that Goldsmith discusses is the case of characteristic tonal melodies that exist independently of the number of syllables of a given word. Goldsmith, citing Leben (1973), notes that Mende, another West African language, has five characteristic tonal patterns. These are:

(91) H   pélé,   kó
      L   bèlè,   kpà
      HL   kényà,   mbû
      LH   nìká,   mbǎ
      LHL   nìkílì,   nyàhâ, mbā

What is interesting here is that the tonal melodies are constant regardless of the number of syllables present. Furthermore, if contour tones surface, they are invariably found on the final syllable of the word. These facts fall out from the postulation of a tonal tier and from the left-to-right association of tones to vowels. For example, the last tonal melody of (91) is L H L. It occurs on words of one, two, or three syllables.

(92)   L H L   L H   L   L H   L
       | | | | | ╱   ╲|╱
       nik il i   nyaha   mba

In the first example, the number of vowels is equal to the number of tones in the melody. Association proceeds from left to right, and each tone is linked to its own vowel. The second form has only two vowels. Having associated the L and H tones to their respective vowels, we still have an extra L to associate. This tone links to the final vowel, forming the observed falling contour tone. In the third case, there is only one vowel. The initial L of the melody is associated to it. The remaining two tones are also linked to it, giving us the double rising-falling contour tone. A glance at the top line of (92) shows that in all three cases the tonal melody is identical. Only the number of syllables found on the segmental tier varies. This clearly illustrates the autonomous nature of the tonal tier.[35]

We have come a long way from the strictly linear representations of SPE. Segments are still represented as matrices of features, but they are organized in terms of syllabic constituents. In the case of tone languages, there is an additional level of structure: the tonal tier. Postulating these additional levels of structure certainly did not solve all the problems of classical generative phonology. Indeed, as might be expected, a new class of problems accompanied each theoretical advance. Certain phenomena, tonal or syllabic, remained recalcitrant. In other cases, predictions made by the respective theories were at variance with the apparent facts. All this is completely normal. What is important is that both syllabic theory and autosegmental theory contributed important restrictions on the expressive power of phonological theory. The conventions of autosegmental theory allow for only certain types of tonal phenomena. A mass of other potential processes are inexpressible in this framework, for example, a process that changes a high tone to a falling tone when followed by a low tone. We have already seen an example of this in the Igbo data. Compare this process to one where a high tone becomes a rising tone before a low tone. In linear phonology, there is no reason to expect to find one phenomenon rather than the other. Both are expressible in feature notation, and both will have about the same cost in these terms. To the credit of autosegmental theory, only the former process is permitted; the latter is deemed impossible. Such a process is inexpressible in autosegmental theory. If all tonal modifications are viewed not as rules, but as local spreading of tones from one vowel to another, there is no way for a high tone to become rising (i.e., a sequence of low–high) *in front of* a low tone. This would require the low tone to creep past the original high tone in order to create a rising tone—the sequence *H L* would have to become *LH L*. This would necessitate crossing the association lines—something that is quite illegal in autosegmental phonology.

To the extent that autosegmental theory is capable of expressing exactly the set of observed tonal phenomena and nothing else, it constitutes an

---

[35]This still leaves open the question of why these melodies rather than five others? The explanatory power of autosegmental theory does have its limits. These limits are explored further in the next chapter.

important step forward in the explanatory power of phonological theory. We have the beginnings of an answer to the question of what is a possible phonological phenomenon? Two levels of structure along with universal principles of association give us an important insight into the organization of phonological representations. Encouraged by the success of these incursions into nonlinear approaches, phonologists naturally looked for a way of extending autosegmental theory to domains other than tone. This search is the subject of the next chapter.

4

Beyond Tones: Extending Nonlinear Phonology

We have come some way from the strictly linear representations of SPE. Syllable structure has been added to the picture. Its exact form and the point at which it is present in a derivation are still subjects of controversy. Its existence and its relevance to phonological processes and the distribution of segments are not. We have seen the splitting of a single level of segmental representation into two distinct tiers: a tonal tier and a segmental tier. We have seen a completely different way of expressing phonological processes: the spreading of association lines. No longer are we limited to the formalism of SPE. No longer are all processes expressed in terms of our familiar canonical rule:

(1) $A \rightarrow B \ /C\underline{\qquad}D$

The formation of contour tones, the propagation of a tone onto an unoccupied segment, the association of tonal affixes are all a significant departure from (1).

There is another major achievement of autosegmental phonology that often passes unnoticed in the literature: It explains the relation between the structural change effectuated by a process and the context in which it occurs. In terms of (1), it explains the connection between B and C____D. Why does a change take place in a given context rather than in some other context? To see this we have only to compare the linear SPE and the nonlinear formulation of some tonal process. Consider the formation of contour tones in Igbo discussed in chapter 3. Recall that the high tone at the end of a noun became a falling tone when followed by a verb with a low tone. Starting with *ékwé à àkhwá,* we get *ékwê à àkhwá.* It is certainly possible to formulate this process in an SPE-type notation. We could say something like:

(2) [+high tone] → [+falling] /_____#[+low tone]

Applying rule (2), or something like it, will indeed derive the correct results. The problem is that there is an arbitrary relation between the matrix to the right of the arrow, [+falling], and the context in which the change takes place, [+low tone]. Even a more perspicacious formulation does not change this fact. If we replace [+falling] by the complex expression [[+high tone][+low tone]], we certainly see a resemblance between the structural change and the context in which it occurs, but the theory treats this as an accident. We could just as easily express a process where no such resemblance appeared in the rule. Our evaluation metric would not reflect the presence or absence of such a resemblance. Phonological rules in the form of (1) treat these resemblances as an accident. Autosegmental theory does not. The same process treated autosegmentally involves the spreading of the low tone on the verb to the preceding final high tone of the noun. Thus, it is no accident that a falling tone is formed where it is. It is precisely the manifestation of the low tone that follows it.

(3) H   H   L   L   H
     | | ╱| | |
     ekwe *cí*   akhwa

A falling tone is a sequence of two tones, H and L, associated with a single vowel. Such a sequence could not arise if a high tone were followed by another high tone; there would be no source for the low tone that is required to form a falling tone. That falling tones are formed before a low tone and not, say, a high tone is a direct consequence of the tenets of autosegmental theory. It is not an accident; it could not happen any other way. Relating a structural change to the context in which it occurs is perhaps the most important contribution of autosegmental theory. Phonological phenomena are no longer random events. It is no longer the case that any segment or class of segments can undergo any change in any context. A phonological process is now expressed by a direct connection of some part of the phonological representation of a neighboring segment. Phonological processes involve, at least in these cases, a sort of binding together of discrete segments. Tones are the mortar of this new kind of structure. This property is particularly significant in view of the discussion in chapter 3 concerning the reasons for the existence of phonological processes in the first place. If we are lucky, form has a lot to say about function.

This leaves us with the following situation: Tonal behavior displays many desirable properties with respect to phonological theory. Many tonal phenomena are amenable to analysis involving association or spreading of tones to given segments. There is a reasoned account as to why these phenomena occur where they do. As for the segments, things are still in the same mess as they were back in the days of SPE. Rules are still formulated in terms of (1). We still do not know why segments undergo the changes they do where they do. It would be lovely if we could apply the same sorts of autosegmental analyses found in tonal phenomena to the more traditional segmental processes. This would, of course, also answer the question of why tones are organized in a different way from all other phonological features. An interesting answer would be that they are not. It should come as no surprise that phonologists armed with autosegmental theory began to have another look at segmental phonology with an eye to extending the former to the latter. Can we find tonal type phenomena at the segmental level? The answer is a resounding yes!

HARMONY

As a graduate student 25 years ago, I began studying a language called Desano, spoken in the northwest Amazon basin. This language does interesting things with nasalization. Simple words seem to be either entirely nasal or entirely oral, and this includes both consonants and vowels. I could find words such as *ba*, where both *b* and *a* are nonnasal (i.e., oral). I could find words such as *mã*, where both *m* and *ã* are nasal. I couldn't find words such as *bã* or *ma*. That is, there seem to be no words that combined oral and nasal segments; it was all one or the other. Nasalization doesn't seem to be associated with individual segments as it is in English. It is rather a property of an entire morpheme. To capture this idea, I decided to write a capital *N* at the end of each nasal morpheme, and nothing after each oral morpheme. I could then write each segment in its oral incarnation.

The vowels were easy. For any nasal vowel, *ṽ*, I wrote *v* for the oral version. The consonants worked out in the following way:[1]

(4) *Oral*   *Nasal*

    b   m

    d   n

---

[1]The oral consonants *b, d, g, γ, w* sound pretty much like their English equivalents in *boy, dog, girl, year,* and *west*. The *r* sound is similar to the American English *t*, as in *pretty*.

The nasal consonants *m* and *n* are like their English counterparts. The velar nasal *ŋ* is like the final *ng* of the word *sing*. The sound *ñ* is roughly like that found in English *canyon*. The nasalized *w, w̃,* is achieved by saying the *w* sound through your nose.

r²	n
g	ŋ
y	ñ
w	w̃

What this means is that a nasalized *b* is an *m*, a nasalized *d*, and *n*, and so on. The voiceless consonants, *p, t, k, s,* and *h* undergo no apparent change in nasal contexts. They occur in either oral or nasal forms. With each segment having a nasal equivalent, I could now write [ba] as *ba* and [mã] as *baN*. The final *N* of *baN* means that all the preceding segments appear in their nasal version: *m* for *b* and *ã* for *a*.

Following the terminology, this was a pretty dippy solution. Why should a nasal symbol *N* have this property? With a bit of hindsight (25 years worth) the answer is clear: The nasal feature displays autosegmental properties quite reminiscent of tones. To make things even more obvious, certain suffixes display two forms: an oral form after oral stems and a nasal form after nasal stems. Don't worry about understanding the values of all these strange symbols. What is important is that the interrogative suffix surfaces as *ri* when following an oral stem, and as *nĩ* when following a nasal stem. Some examples follow:

(5)   −ri/−nĩ *'interrogative suffix'*
              Oral Stems

wa'a 'to go'   wa'ari 'do (you) go?'
baya 'to dance'   bayari 'do (you) dance?'
yi'ɨ 'I'   yi'ɨri 'me?'

              Nasal Stems

õã 'to be well'   õãnĩ 'are (you) well?'
mãsĩ 'to know'   mãsĩnĩ 'do (you) know?'
mĩ'ɨ 'you'   mĩ'ɨnĩ 'you?'

Remember the toneless suffix −*le* that I presented in chapter 3. I repeat the relevant forms in (6).

(6)

	klá̰	'to chop down'	kla	'to grab'
Imperfective	klá̰-lé	'chops down with'	kla-le	'grabs with'
Perfective	klá̰-lè	'chopped down with'	klà-lè	'grabbed with'

___
²[r] is really just a variant of *d*. [r] is found only in the middle of words. [d] occurs in initial position.

Here, the tone of the suffix of the imperfective forms is identical to the tone of the stem: mid-high when the stem is mid-high and mid when the stem is mid. In the Desano case, just replace the tone by a nasal feature and the results are the same: nasal suffix after nasal stem, oral suffix after oral stem. Suppose that segments are oral unless we indicate the contrary (i.e., their unmarked form is non-nasal). Now either a stem carries a nasal autoseg-ment, which I will represent as N, or it has nothing at all. In the latter case, the segment will be interpreted as oral because this is the default case. Let's take two stems, one oral and one nasal, and apply to them this autosegmen-tal representation.

(7) *Nasal Tier*   N

     Segmental Tier   b a y a │ b a s i

The stem *baya* is oral and so has nothing at the nasal level. The stem [mãsĩ] is a nasal stem. An *N* appears on the nasal tier. The segmental tier contains the oral version of each segment. What happens next? We apply the same association conventions that we did in the case of tones. A nasal autosegment, if one occurs, is linked in a one-to-one, left-to-right manner. Unlike the tones, which only link to vowels, the nasal autosegment links to every segment. This is shown in (8).

(8) *Nasal Tier*   N

     Segmental Tier   b a y a │ b a s i

Nothing happens in the case of *baya* because there is no autosegment to link to the elements on the segmental tier. In the case of [mãsĩ], the nasal autosegment begins by linking with the left-most segment *b*. Because there are no other autosegments around, it continues to associate with all the remaining segments, yielding an entirely nasal morpheme. Aside from the stipulation that the nasal autosegment associates to both consonants and vowels, we have changed absolutely nothing from our autosegmental tonal analyses. It's the same theory. Handling the oral/nasal alternations of the suffix is strictly child's play.

(9) *Nasal Tier*   N

     Segmental Tier   b a y a + ri │ b a s i + r i

In the case of [bayari], the interrogative suffix must be realized orally. There is no nasal autosegment associated with the stem and the suffix itself has none. In the second case, things are different. The nasal autosegment that makes up part of the lexical representation of the verb *to know* extends itself to the suffix. It links to both the consonant *r* and the vowel *i*. Now, we have changed the representations of segments. Before, a consonant such as *m* was simply a feature matrix. Now, *m* has the same representation as *b*, with the addition of the nasal autosegment. In like manner, *i* is a feature matrix and *ī* is this same feature matrix accompanied by the nasal autosegment. This is something like saying that $b + N = $ [m] and $i + N = $ [ĩ].

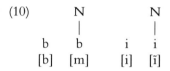

Two questions immediately come to mind: Is the nasal autosegment simply the feature [+nasal]? Are nasal segments represented as in (10) in every language? Most phonologists would answer "yes" to the first question and "no" to the second. I happen to disagree on both points, but I discuss that later. Because features are still generally believed to be the ultimate constituents of phonological segments, it is natural to assume that autosegments were also composed of these units. Until the mid 1970s, there was no real choice. Symbols such as H, L, and N were simply abbreviations for the more orthodox features or feature matrices, just as the symbols *b* or *i* are abbreviations for feature matrices.

Nasalization apparently does not display autosegmental properties in every language, thus it was assumed that it did not occupy its own tier in every language. The normal or unmarked case [nasal] behaved like any other feature and was grouped with its peers in the matrices of the segmental tier. On some occasions, it might be liberated from this tier, that is, in some cases [nasal] was autosegmentalized. When such an event occurred, as in Desano, [nasal] was no longer to be represented on the segmental tier. It came to occupy its own nasal tier and there it displayed its classic autosegmental properties. In other words, at least in some cases nasalization acts like tones do. Thus, autosegmental theory is not limited to tonal phenomena.

Nasalization is not at all unique in its manifestation of autosegmental properties. Cases of vowel harmony were well known and were soon receiving autosegmental treatment.[3] It is easy to understand what vowel harmony is. The Desano nasal harmony described earlier provides a good introduction to it. In many languages, there are restrictions on what vowels can occur with what other vowels within some domain, such as the word.

---

[3]Indeed, harmonic phenomena were treated nonlinearly back in the 1940s, considerably before the birth of autosegmental theory. (Cf. Waterson, 1956.)

The difference between the Desano phenomenon, which I can now call *nasal harmony*, and the more traditional harmonic systems is that the latter generally (but by no means always) applied only to vowels and involved features such as [back], [round], and [tense].[4]

Let's return to a now familiar language: Vata. Vata has two sets of vowels: [+ATR] and [−ATR]. Typically, only members of the same set are found together in a word. In the following examples, [−ATR] vowels will be represented with lowercase symbols, [+ATR] vowels with uppercase. Vata has a system of 10 vowels: 5 [−ATR] (represented here as a, e, i, o, u) and 5 [+ATR] (represented as A, E, I, O, U).

(11)   *The Vata vowel System*

[−ATR]		[+ATR]	
i	u	I	U
e	o	E	O
	a		A

The exact phonetic differences between these sets of vowels is not essential to the understanding of the formal nature of the harmony process. Suffice it to say that a phonetic property, labeled ATR, distinguishes them. For convenience, I have transcribed all vowels possessing this property in uppercase and all vowels lacking it, in lowercase. The symbols used are, of course, irrelevant. They merely reflect the phonetic similarity within the two sets of vowels. As I mentioned earlier, Vata words contain vowels drawn exclusively from one set or the other. There is no mixing of [+ATR] vowels with [−ATR] vowels. Unlike nasalization in the Desano example, ATR-ness is a property restricted to vowels. It has no apparent consequences for consonants. Examples of ATR harmony can be seen in the following examples:[5]

(12)   [−ATR]   [+ATR]

lete	'iron'	mEnA	'nose'
neni	'walk'	kOsU	'fire'
golu	'canoe'	bIdO	'wash'

---

[4]This last feature is sometimes referred to as [ATR] in the literature, meaning advanced tongue root. [+ATR] or [+tense] vowels involve greater muscular tension in their articulation as well as an expansion of the pharyngeal cavity created by moving the root of the tongue forward in the mouth. No intimate knowledge of the feature is required in order to follow the discussion. It is sometimes said to characterize the difference between *e* in *red* ([−tense]) and *ai* in *raid*, among other things.

[5]For clarity, I have not included tonal markings on the vowels. This harmony is completely independent of tonal phenomena.

Only vowels drawn from the same set may cooccur. The reader should note that only vowels of the same class ([+ATR] or [−ATR]) may cooccur. No mixing of vowels from the two classes is allowed. Forms such as *lEto or *kosA are ill formed in Vata. By now, we have enough experience with autosegmental phenomena not to hesitate an instant. Vata ATR harmony bears a strong resemblance to the tonal processes discussed earlier and to Desano nasal harmony. All we need to do now is decide which of the two values of [ATR] is the default case. There is considerable evidence that [−ATR] is the unmarked value of this feature. Following our now established procedure, all vowels will be assumed to be [−ATR] unless there are indications to the contrary. These indications will take the form of an association line linking vowels to the ATR autosegment, which I will represent as *Atr*. Accordingly, the [−ATR] vowel *a* will be distinguished from its [+ATR], *A* counterpart as shown in (13).

(13)   [−ATR]   [+ATR]

   ATR Tier   Atr
                                     |

   Segmental Tier   a   a
                          [a]   [A]

All we need to do is apply the Desano analysis of nasal harmony to Vata. We must stipulate that only vowels can bear the ATR autosegment. Some morphemes will contain the ATR autosegment, others will not. In the former case, ATR will display normal autosegmental behavior and link to every vowel in its domain starting from the left. Thus, in words with several vowels, all will be produced with the same value for the feature [ATR]: [+ATR] if the autosegment is present and [−ATR] if it is not. A mixed morpheme is inexpressible in this formalism. This is a lovely result because mixed morphemes hardly ever occur.[6] The representations for multivowel morphemes are given in (14).

(14) [−ATR]   [+ATR]

              Atr
              |\

    g o l u   k o s u
    [golu]   [kOsU]

---

[6]Of course, we need a way to override the normal autosegmental linking conventions to handle those mixed cases that do exist. There are a number of ways of doing this, but they do not interest us here.

By now it should come as no surprise to learn that if we tack on a suffix, it will surface with the same value for the feature [ATR] as the preceding stem. If the ATR autosegment is present, it will simply continue its journey rightward, associating to the vowel of the suffix. If there is no autosegment on the stem, there is nothing to spread and the vowel of the suffix retains its default value, namely [−ATR]. All this is shown in (15).

(15) kla 'to cut down'   ll 'to eat'   −lo 'passive suffix'

<pre>
                             Atr
                             |\
    k l a l o   l i l o
    [klalo] 'be cut down'   [lIlO] 'be eaten'
</pre>

What emerges from all this is that autosegmental behavior is by no means limited to tones. We now have all kinds of features popping up here and there in various languages displaying these kind of properties. The picture of phonological representations is now much richer. There are several levels or tiers. Units occupying different tiers may be linked by association lines. Each tier may undergo certain types of changes. In the normal case, no other tier is affected. The results of such changes are manifested by relinking. Perhaps a nagging doubt remains. Tones seem so different from features such as [ATR]. The latter have always been associated with inherent properties of vocalic segments. Tones, on the other hand, have been traditionally transcribed with accent marks. This leaves us with the impression that they are indeed somehow external to the basic quality of the vowel with which they are associated. An *á* with a high tone is still an *a*. It is less obvious that an *i* that is [+ATR] is still the same animal. Using more familiar vowels, languages such as Turkish and Hungarian have a system of vowel harmony involving the feature [back]. In such languages, suffixes are found whose vowel is *a* when preceded by a [+back] stem and *e* when preceded by a [−back] stem. It is very hard to believe that an *e* is a kind of *a* (or, if you wish, vice versa) in the same sense that an *é* or an *è* is a kind of *e*. It would seem strange to symbolize an *e* as an *a* with some kind of accent mark.[7] The clincher seems to be that we can remove a vowel out from under a tone and yet the tone can continue to exist. Could we get rid of a vowel out from under an ATR autosegment, leaving the latter free to associate elsewhere? These cases would certainly go a long way toward convincing us that tonal behavior really is present in more segmentally

---

[7]In fact, it is not all that strange. German represents some [e]s as *ä*, as in *räder* 'wheels'. These vowels are the result of a historic process called *umlaut*, which is yet another type of harmony process.

oriented features. And in fact we have just such a case in Vata. We can really eliminate a vowel that has an ATR autosegment, and this autosegment escapes unscathed. I proceed with the demonstration.

To this point, I have only talked about harmony within the word. Vata also has an optional harmony process that goes across word boundaries. This is a directional process subject to a number of interesting conditions, which I don't go into here. Suffice it to say that the ATR autosegment may spread from one word to the final syllable of the word to its left. A typical environment for this directional harmony is a subject pronoun followed by a verb. In the following examples, you see that the subject pronoun, normally produced with a [−ATR] vowel, may be pronounced with a [+ATR] vowel if the following verb is [+ATR].

(16) o   la 'he calls'   O lE 'he eats'
      he call   he eat

      wa   zo 'they put'   wA nO 'they hear'
      they put   they hear

It is quite straightforward to account for these data. The autosegments associated with the verbs in the right column spread to the pronoun found immediately to their left. To complete the demonstration we need to look at a second process. I have to express this process in the traditional terms of generative phonology. We see later that this process, too, can be expressed in autosegmental terms. In Vata, a nonhigh vowel assimilates completely to an immediately following vowel. I can illustrate this process by again using verbs and pronouns. This time I use object pronouns instead of the subject pronouns seen in (16). Vata has six third person pronouns: *i, u, e, o, a,* and *wa.* The different pronouns refer to the different noun classes that exist in Vata. The choice of the pronoun depends on the identity of the noun to which it refers. This is something like the situation in French, where there are three object pronouns: *le* for masculine singular nouns, *la* for feminine singular nouns, and *les* for plural nouns. We can say, *Je le vois* 'I see him/it' when referring to someone male or to some object that happens to have masculine gender in French (e.g., a wall). The sentence *Je la vois* 'I see her/it' can refer to someone female or to some object having feminine gender (e.g., a table). *Je les vois* 'I see them' has the pronoun *les,* which can refer to anything plural—be it animate or inanimate. Vata is just like French except it has more classes or genders than French. Aside from the pronoun *o,* which is used for people (sex is not distinguished), the other pronouns are pretty arbitrary. I translate them by the English pronoun *it* or *them.* With the preliminaries out of the way, let's get to the examples.

(17) *Verbs*   zo 'put'   nO 'hear'

    Pronoun

      i   zo + i = zii 'put them'   nO + i = nii 'hear them'
      u   zo + u = zuu 'put it'   nO + u = nuu 'hear it'
      e   zo + e = zee 'put it'   nO + e = nee 'hear it'
      o   zo + o = zoo 'put it'   nO + o = noo 'hear it'
      a   zo + a = zaa 'put it'   nO + a = naa 'hear it'

In each case, the first vowel of the two-vowel sequence becomes identical to the second. This includes the feature [ATR]. The object pronouns are all [−ATR], therefore the final vowels of the verb stems all surface as [−ATR] as well. This is true whether they start out [−ATR], as in *zo*, or [+ATR], as in *nO*. The resulting sequences are identical for the two verbs. But what about the ATR autosegment that started out with the verb *hear*? It appears to have disappeared completely, but has it? We now enter the crucial phase of our experiment. There is a way of finding out if the ATR autosegment has been lost along with the rest of the first vowel of the sequence. All we have to do is place a subject pronoun in front of the forms in (17). Recall that the ATR autosegment, if present, spreads from the verb to a subject pronoun (cf. the forms of (16)). If the ATR autosegment really behaves like a tone, it should make its presence felt when the subject pronoun is added. I use the forms [zaa] 'put it' and [naa] 'hear it', and the subject pronoun *o* 'he/she' for this experiment.

(18) a. o zo 'he/she puts'   O nO 'he/she hears'
      b. o zaa 'he/she puts it'   O naa 'he/she hears it'

The forms of (18a) are supplied as a reminder of the nature of the harmony process. The subject pronoun becomes [+ATR] if the following verb stem is [+ATR]. What really interests us are the forms of (18b). Before the verb-object complex [zaa], the pronoun remains [−ATR]. This is to be expected; *zo* itself is [−ATR]. But look at the form [naa]. The vowel sequence is pronounced in exactly the same way as that of [zaa]. There is no phonetic difference. The subject pronoun harmonizes just as if the vowel of the following verb stem were [+ATR]. In fact, the vowels that appear are [aa], both [−ATR]. Something not associated with this vowel sequence must have caused the subject pronoun to change; we get [O naa] and not [o naa]. This mysterious agent must be the ATR autosegment cut loose after the assimilation of its vowel.

Because we return to this and similar examples later on, let me present the story step-by-step. We begin with the initial representation shown in (19).[8]

(19) *a.* *Lexical Form*

    Atr
     |
  o   no   a
  subj. hear obj.
  pron.   pron.

b. *Assimilation*

    Atr

  o   na   a

c. *Direction Harmony*

    Atr
    /
  o   na   a

d. *Phonetic Form*
  [O naa]

In (19a), we see the starting point. We have a verb stem with an associated autosegment preceded by a subject pronoun and followed by an object pronoun. Neither of the pronouns is [+ATR], that is, neither is associated with an ATR autosegment. The assimilation process applies in (19b). The final vowel of the verb becomes identical to the vowel of the following pronoun. This involves the loss of the vowel *o* but not the autosegment with which it was linked. This latter element is cut loose and floats above the segmental tier. We have seen that an autosegment associated with a verb will spread leftward onto a preceding syllable. In (19c), we see that this occurs even if the autosegment is no longer attached to its verb stem. The vowel of the subject pronoun is now linked to ATR and is realized as a [+ATR] vowel [O]. The phonetic form given in (19d) has been correctly derived.

The point of this exercise was to show that many features, normally associated with the segmental tier, do indeed manifest behavior reminiscent of tones. The good news is that more and more processes, traditionally viewed as segmental, come to be treated autosegmentally. As we have seen, autosegmental processes are much more constrained than those based on SPE-type rules. The formal devices utilized by autosegmental theory are putting two things together (creating an association line) or pulling two

---

[8]The true nature of (19b)—assimilation—is revealed later on. In reality, it involves the loss of the first vowel of the sequence.

things apart (deleting an association line). We have taken an enormous step forward in explanatory power. Rules can pretty well describe any conceivable phenomenon. Even with the addition of markedness theory, the expressive power of a phonological rule far exceeds anything known to exist in human phonological systems. On the other hand, taking the extreme (and, in my view, the correct) position that all phonological phenomena can be described in terms of putting things together or taking them apart cuts down enormously on what can be expressed as a phonological process. To the extent that the greatly reduced set of phenomena allowed for by autosegmental theory are precisely those observed in phonological systems, we are justified in believing that this theory, or something like it, underlies human linguistic competence. This is not to say that we are anywhere near a complete or adequate theory of phonology. A considerable number of problems, many of a fundamental nature, remain. What is encouraging is that the nature of our problems are completely reversed. In classical generative phonology, we had no difficulty in expressing any phonological process that came across our path. What was troubling was the equal ease with which we could formulate processes that by general agreement were absolutely impossible. In short, classical generative phonology suffered from a formal structure that was insufficiently restrictive. It was possible to write absolute nonsense using this theory.

The point I am making here is that the distinction between linear and nonlinear phonology is not merely notational. A phonological theory contains, among other things, a representational scheme for defining the objects and events within its domain. The representational scheme sets limits for what is expressible. The theory that incorporates a given representational scheme is making the claim that events that are inexpressible *do not exist*. It should be clear that the SPE system, with its rules, and autosegmental theory, where events are limited to the sort of spreading we have seen, are not equivalent in their expressive power. Concretely, there is no logical or necessary connection between the structural change effectuated by an SPE-type rule and the context in which it occurs. The fact that a segment becomes nasal in the immediate environment of another nasal is treated as an accident in this theory.

With the birth of more restrictive theories, the pendulum is swinging the other way. In a constrained autosegmental theory, it is much more difficult, if not impossible, to express nonsensical processes. Apparent problems for this theory involve observed phenomena that surpass its descriptive power. I regard this as a much healthier situation. In time we may find out (this has already happened in certain cases) that the so-called counterexamples to the theory are only illusions. They may be based on false assumptions, faulty or incomplete data, or simply temporarily beyond the limits of a theory that is obviously incomplete.

In sum, the study of tonal phenomena showed that linear approaches to phonology, such as SPE, offered unsatisfactory solutions. The more constrained nonlinear approaches, such as autosegmental theory, provided principled accounts for how and why observed phenomena occur in the way that they do. Nonlinear theories have the further advantage of drastically reducing the set of possible phonological processes. The fit between the theoretical and the observed range of phenomena is good enough for us to be encouraged to extend this approach to more and more areas of phonology. With this in mind, let's return to the syllable.

SYLLABIC PROCESSES

In chapter 3's section on speculations about phonological processes, I presented the outlines of a theory of syllable structure. The motivation for using syllable structure in contexts of phonological processes was given later in that chapter, in the section entitled Enter the Syllable. The arguments for including syllabic information in phonological representations were made in the framework of linear phonology. It remains to be seen if syllable structure in general and syllable constituents in particular display the kinds of autosegmental behavior that we have found in other aspects of phonological representations. Tree structures have been used to indicate membership of a segment in a particular syllabic constituent. A segment is thus linked to a constituent. Such structures are potential candidates for the kind of treatment we have given to tonal and harmonic phenomena. What we need to know is whether syllable structures have an autosegmental character. Put another way, can the postulation of syllable structure allow us to remove yet another class of phenomena from the cruel grip of SPE-type rule notation. To find out, let's look at one type of process that is directly related to syllable constituent structure.

Many languages of the world display an alternation between a high vowel and its corresponding glide.[9] French is one of these languages. This change, when it occurs, takes place invariably before another vowel. The SPE-type rule for the process, which has the high vowel as its starting point, is shown in (20).

(20) *Devocalizaiton*

$$\begin{bmatrix} +\text{syll} \\ +\text{high} \end{bmatrix} \rightarrow [-\text{syll}] / \underline{\qquad} [+\text{syll}]$$

I am assuming, as is customary, that only the value of the feature [syll] distinguishes a high vowel from its corresponding glide. Thus, [i] and [y]

---

[9]Glides, also known as semivowels or semiconsonants, are represented in English by the segments *w* and *y*, as in *win* and *young.*

share all the same feature specifications except that the former is [+syll], whereas the latter is [−syll]. Rule (20) states that any high vowel immediately followed by another vowel will change into its corresponding glide: *i* will become *y*, *u* will become *w*, *ü* will become *ẅ*, and so on. Again, rule (20) does not tell us why such a change takes place before another vowel rather than, say, before any [+coronal], any [+nasal], or any other imaginable context. The fact that this devocalization takes place before another vowel is treated as an accident. The problem is that it is an accident that happens in phonological systems all over the world. This process shows up in French, as seen in the following examples:

(21) si   *scie*   'saws'   sye   *scier*   'to saw'
      avu   *avoue*   'admits'   avwe   *avouer*   'to admit'
      tü   *tue*   'kills'   tẅe   *tuer*   'to kill'

In (21), I present three verbs, all of which end in a high vowel. This vowel is in word-final position in the forms of the column on the left. In this position, it is pronounced as a vowel. In the fourth column, I give the infinitival form of each verb. Regular French verbs form their infinitives by adding the suffix [e], spelled *er*. The high vowels then appear in two contexts: in word-final position and followed by a vowel. It is this latter context that triggers the devocalization rule (20) and accounts for the presence of the glides in the infinitival form.

In fact, there is an autosegmental treatment for this phenomenon that involves syllable structure and requires nothing like rule (20).[10] Suppose, oversimplifying somewhat, we assume that a high vowel and its corresponding glide are really the same thing. The perceived difference between, say, and *i* and a *y* can be attributed entirely to their syllabic position. The high vowel variant occurs in the syllabic nucleus; the glide variant occurs elsewhere. This allows us to get rid of the feature [syll]. Its presence is a bit of an embarrassment given the fact that syllable structure must be present in phonological representations. We say that the syllabicity of a segment is not an inherent property but rather follows directly from the position in syllable structure in which the segment is found. To avoid confusion, I will use new symbols for the segments that now combine high vowel and glide incarnations: *I* for [i] and [y], *U* for [u] and [w], and *Ü* for [ü] and [ẅ]. The difference between [i] and [y] will now look something like (22).

(22) *Syllable Tier*   N   O
                          | |
      Segmental Tier   I   I
                         [i] [y]

---

[10]Here, I follow the analysis presented in Kaye and Lowenstamm (1984).

The vowel on the left is associated with the constituent N (= nucleus) and so receives a syllabic interpretation. On the right, I have chosen an onset (O) as a nonnuclear context. In this case, the segment *I* receives a non-syllabic interpretation, namely [y]. What is crucial is that there is no difference between these two sounds at the segmental level. They differ only with respect to their syllabic position.

Now let's apply this idea to the French examples. Consider the two forms *scie* and *scier*.

(23) a. O N   b. O N N
        | | | | |
        s I   s I e

(23a) represents the form *scie* (= [si]). The *s* forms the onset of the syllable and the nucleus containing *I* follows. *I* is in the nucleus and therefore receives a syllabic interpretation, which we note as [i]. In (23b), we find the same stem followed by the infinitival suffix *-e*. This suffix consists of a single vowel, which is the nucleus of the following syllable. No consonant separates these two nuclei and so no onset occurs between them. If nothing happened to change the form of (23b), we would expect it to be pronounced as two syllables: *si – e*. Indeed, some speakers of French pronounce this form in exactly this way. More commonly, however, the monosyllabic pronunciation [sye] is what is produced. In (23b), two consecutive nuclei occur on the syllabic tier.

It turns out that this is a very precarious structure, one that is eschewed in many languages. Suppose we say the following:

(24) In French, delete the first of two consecutive nuclei.

(24) can be thought of as a stipulation for the time being. In fact, it follows from a very general principle that involves identical elements occurring at *any level of structure* and not just the syllabic tier. More is said about this later. For the moment, let's just suppose that the first of the two successive nuclei gets removed from the structure. This leaves us with (25).

(25) O   N
     | |
     s I   e

What we have done is cut loose the segment *I* from the syllabic tier. This *I* is now floating. As we have seen in both tonal and harmonic phenomena, a floating element is going to look for some place to dock. In (25), there are two logical possibilities. It can link to the onset to its left, or it can link to the nucleus to its right. In fact, we can predict where the *I* will go but that would be getting us way ahead of our story. Let me just stipulate that the *I* will associate to its left. This yields the structure in (26).

(26) O   N
      |\ |
      s I   e

The segment *I* is now part of the onset. We know that a nonnuclear *I* is the glide [y]. (26) is the structure that underlies the pronunciation [sye]. We have succeeded in explaining what happens when an [i] changes into a [y] (as well as the other high vowel–glide alternations shown in (21)) and why it happens precisely where it does. We have made two stipulations: Languages don't like sequences of nuclei, and the floating segment associates to the left rather than to the right. As I mentioned earlier, we can derive both of these stipulations from general, independently motivated principles of phonological theory. What started out as an arbitrary rule in (20) is now almost completely derivable from general principles. Furthermore, we see that syllable structure is involved in the same types of autosegmental behavior as are tones and harmonic features.

But things get even better! Further study of French verbs reveals an interesting fact: No devocalization takes place if the high vowel is immediately preceded by an consonant–liquid cluster. Compare the following forms:

(27) pli *plie* 'folds'   pliye *plier*   'to fold'   *plye
      tru *troue* 'digs'   truwe *trouer* 'to dig'   *trwe
      glü *glu*   'glue'   glüw̃ã *gluant* 'sticky'   *glw̃ã

The examples of (27) do not seem to follow the normal pattern. Adding the infinitival suffix *-e* to *pli* does not yield the expected *[plye] (cf. *si* plus *-e* = [sye]). The result is [pliye]. The same holds for the remaining examples. I have chosen a noun as the third form of (27), but this should make no difference. We would expect the suffix *-ant* to behave like *-er*, and indeed it does in such forms as *sciant* 'sawing' [sy̰ã]. Note further that a glide mysteriously appears between the final stem vowel and suffix vowel. For example, the failure of devocalization to apply does not yield simply [plie]; the result is [pliye]. We have two questions to answer: Why doesn't the stem vowel change into a glide as before? Where does the additional glide separating the two vowels come from?

If we were back in the SPE era, we could account for the failure of rule (2) to apply by adding an additional condition to its context. The result would look something like (28).

(28) *Devocalization—New Version*

$$\begin{bmatrix} +\text{syll} \\ +\text{high} \end{bmatrix} \rightarrow [-\text{syll}] \ / \sim [\text{C Liq}] \underline{\quad\quad} [+\text{syll}]$$

Rule (28) contains the Boolean negation operator ~. It can be satisfied by any string that does not match the expression enclosed in brackets. In other words, rule (28) will apply as long as the vowel which is to undergo it is not preceded by a consonant followed by a liquid. Once again, a rule-based treatment treats this fact as an accident. The argument of the operator could have been any other conceivable expression. One could equally query the necessity of Boolean operators themselves in the contexts of phonological rules, but let us leave that question aside.[11]

The expression [C Liq] has a familiar ring to it. In fact, we have seen it crop up repeatedly in the context of our discussion on syllable structure. Consonants and liquids, in that order, are precisely the segments that can form a branching onset. Can this be a coincidence? In fact, the data of (27) are a direct consequence of the theory of the syllable already presented. To see why, let's consider the infinitive *plier* and follow its derivation. Its lexical representation follows:

(29)   O   N   N
       |\ | |
       p l   i   e

The first of the two consecutive nuclei is eliminated, cutting loose the associated *i*.

(30)   O   N
       |\ |
       p l   i   e

The floating *i* will now try to dock somewhere, but where? It can't link to the onset; this would create an impossible structure, as shown in (31).

(31)   O   N
        / | \ |
       p l i   e

---

[11]The reader will recall that in our discussion of the analysis of English stress, the utilization of such negative contexts was symptomatic of a faulty analysis.

Associating the *i* to the onset position creates an onset with three segments. Syllable theory limits each constituent to a maximum of two segments. The structure of (31) is impossible. What is going on is really quite simple. For one reason or another, nuclear sequences are unstable. Derivations lead to their elimination in one way or another. One solution is to remove a vocalic segment from one of the nuclei and place it into the onset. But if the onset is already saturated—if it is branching—this move is impossible. We can't wind up with an onset that has three segments. Syllable theory then predicts that French devocalization cannot take place following a branching onset (i.e., following a consonant–liquid sequence). This prediction if confirmed by the data in (27). Indeed, the French facts provide a striking confirmation to the theory of syllable structure and its relevance to a number of phonological processes. Far from complicating the situation, as is the case in a rule-based approach (cf. rules (20) and (28)), the facts of (21) and (27) could not be otherwise, given the theory of syllable structure presented earlier. In this sense, syllable theory *explains* why high vowels do not devocalize following consonant–liquid sequences.

It may be argued that the French facts offer no reason to posit such abstract and unobservable constructs as syllabic constituents. A more concrete approach might suggest that the failure to transform high vowels into glides is simply a superficial, phonetically motivated constraint against the creation of sequences that are difficult to pronounce. After all, it is reasonable to suppose that it is easier to pronounce the sequence [vw], as in [avwe] *avouer,* than it is to produce the sequence [trw], which is what we would have to do if devocalization applied to a form such as *tru + e.* In other words, sequences consisting of a consonant, a liquid, and a glide are too difficult to occur, at least in French. This explanation sounds plausible enough and doesn't involve appealing to abstract entities such as syllable constituents. Both theories seem to make the same predictions and so we can use Occam's razor to slice syllable structure from our explanation of French devocalization.

There is only one problem with all this: Consonant–liquid–glide sequences are quite frequent in French. The following examples illustrate such sequences:

(32) *French Consonant–Liquid–Glide Sequences*

trois	'three' [trwa]	pluie 'rain'	[plẅi]
emploi	'job' [ãplwa]	truite 'trout'	[trẅit]
croix	'cross' [krwa]	bruit 'noise'	[brẅi]

Consider the form *trouer.* If the production of a consonant–liquid–vowel cluster is so difficult that we must say [truwe] rather than *[trwe], why does it suddenly become easier when we pronounce the word *trois?* This word can only be pronounced [trwa] and never as *[truwa]. Obviously, French speakers are capable of producing the sequence [trw], so an inability to do so cannot be the reason that devocalization fails to apply to a form such as *trouer*. The phonetic explanation founders on the rocks of the data. But let's not be too quick to pat ourselves on the back. Granted that there is no obvious phonetic explanation for these facts, can the syllable-based theory do any better? After all, it excludes onsets containing three segments. Now a word such as *trois* [trwa] begins with the sequence *trw*. Doesn't this mean that syllable theory is wrong? If this were true, the entire explanation for forms such as *trouer* would collapse, and syllable theory would be in just as much trouble as the phonetically based theory. The answer is that a form such as *trois* [trwa] has only two consonants in its onset, *t* and *r*. One immediately wonders where the *w* is going to go. The answer is that the *w* is in the nucleus and not in the onset. To convince you that this is true, I need to discuss the missing link of phonological representations. As you might well imagine, this missing link is in the form of a skeleton.

THE SKELETON COMES OUT OF THE CLOSET

In the previous section, we saw that syllable structure may play an important role in the understanding of some phonological processes. Specifically, syllable constituents display autosegmental behavior of the now familiar type. They are linked to elements by the same sorts of association lines that we encountered in tonal and harmonic phenomena. Until now I have been assuming that syllabic constituents were linked directly to phonological segments. In fact, we shall see that this assumption is incorrect. I begin with a discussion of some of the problems associated with this assumption.

Linking Segments to Syllabic Constituents:
The Problems

Our story leads us to the consideration of some data from the dialect of Dida spoken around the town of Lakota in the Ivory Coast.[12] Dida is very closely related to Vata, a language with which we are now quite familiar. I again look at sequences of verbs followed by object pronouns. In many cases, Vata and Dida differ only in the tones associated with the given morphemes. The reader is advised to refer back to the section on harmony

---

[12]I summarize the results that appeared in Kaye and Charette (1981). The original idea of a level of representation intervening between segments and syllable structure is found in McCarthy (1979). His work is based on data from Semitic languages.

in this chapter for a quick reminder concerning the forms and processes to be discussed.

Dida contains a number of verbs that occur with a mid-high tone in imperfective forms. For reasons that become clear anon, I choose two such verbs: one with a nonhigh vowel, pá 'throw'; and another with a high vowel, jú 'put'.[13] Dida, like Vata, has a process in which a nonhigh vowel completely assimilates to an immediately following vowel. Verb–object pronoun sequences provide a context in which this process applies. I use the pronoun ó 'him/her' in these examples, but any other pronoun would have done as well.

(33) pá ó 'throws him' [póó]   jú ó 'puts her' [júó]

In the first example, the stem vowel á assimilates completely to the following suffix vowel ó. The result is a sequence of two distinct ós. In the second case, the stem vowel is high and thus not subject to the assimilation process. No changes take place and we hear the sequence úó as two distinct syllables. A nice way to treat the assimilation process is simply to delete the initial vowel of the sequence while leaving the syllable structure intact. Following our normal autosegmental conventions, the now liberated nucleus should look for a handy vowel to link onto. In the example at hand, ó is the only available vowel. Linking takes place and now the single segment ó is realized on two successive nuclei.[14] This produces exactly the desired results. [póó] contains a sequence of two nuclei containing the same vowel. The (simplified) derivation follows:

(34) a. *Initial Representation*

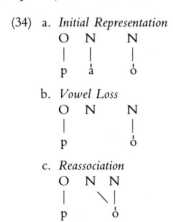

 b. *Vowel Loss*

 c. *Reassociation*

---

[13]I follow the convention adopted for the Vata data: Lowercase symbols represent [−ATR] vowels and uppercase symbols represent [+ATR] vowels.

[14]I have mentioned that nuclear sequences are unstable. Dida is one language that preserves them, at least in certain cases. Changes do occur, however, as we see here.

This way of looking at assimilation has a lot going for it. It fully exploits the autosegmental properties of syllable structure. It conforms to a restricted theory of phonological processes, which involves either putting things together or pulling them apart. Eliminating the first vowel segment comes under the heading of pulling things apart. Assimilation then does not require any new mechanism. It can be handled in a standard autosegmental way. What appears to be a change in a segment is in reality the loss of the segment, but not of its syllabic position (the nucleus), and the subsequent filling of this now empty position by an available segment (the remaining vowel). The assimilation process is now reduced to the desired level of formal simplicity. In the case of the verb *jú* 'puts', nothing happens at all. The vowel is not deleted and our output is identical to our input.

(35)   O   N   N
       | | |
       j   ú   ò

Verbs can occur in forms other than the imperfective. In particular, there is the imperative form. The difference between the two forms involves a tonal change for the verbs we have been using. Whereas the imperfective form has a mid-high tone, the imperative form has a high tone. The startling fact is that this tonal change also produces dramatic differences in our vowel sequences. The data are given in (36).

(36)   a. pá 'throw!'   pá + ò pó 'throw him!'
       b. jú 'put!'   jú + ò juǒ 'put her!'
       c. jú 'put!'   jú + ú jú 'put it!'

What a difference a tone makes! The imperfective form *pá* plus the pronoun *ò* yielded [póò], with two distinct vowels. The imperative form *pá* plus the same pronoun *ò* yields *pó* with a single vowel. In (36b), wee see the same result when applied to a high vowel. Here, the two segments are retained but the result is not a sequence of two vowels. It is a diphthong, that is, two vowel segments are pronounced as a single unit occupying a single nucleus. This is similar to the vowel in *pure,* where a [yu] sequence occupies a single nuclear position and behaves as a unit. I get to the form in (36c) a bit later. Let's take stock of the situation. In the case of the imperfective forms, we simply lost the first of two successive vowels if it was nonhigh. Nothing else was changed. The imperative forms of (36) are different. Not only have we lost a vowel segment, exactly as before, but the resulting sequence has been simplified to a single nuclear position. This is realized as a simple vowel if we lost the first vowel (i.e., if the first vowel was nonhigh) or as a diphthong (two vowel segments occupying a single nucleus) if the first vowel was high. In all cases, the first nucleus was eliminated. Furthermore, we also lost our mid-high tone that appeared on the pronoun. The remaining nucleus, be it simple or diphthongal, bears only a high tone. No trace of the mid-high tone remains.

It is at this point that one must resist the temptation to panic. Things aren't really that complicated. This example is a lovely illustration of how autosegmental representations work. Things are deleted on the various levels, and what remains reassociates in a proper autosegmental way. We must remind ourselves that phonological processes are just putting things together or pulling them apart. In this case, we are dealing, simultaneously, with three different levels: a segmental level, a syllabic level, and a tonal level. The segmental level is easy; we've already seen it work in the imperfective forms. We know that a nonhigh vowel will delete before another vowel. This was true before and it remains true in the imperative examples.

What about the tones? Well, we started out with a sequence of two tones: a high tone on the imperative form of the verb and a mid-high tone on the object pronoun. The end result is a high tone. Therefore, a mid-high tone must be eliminated when it follows a high tone. Finally, consider the syllabic nuclei. In the imperative forms, we started out with two nuclei: one in the verb and the other in the pronoun. We wind up with one nucleus. Conclusion: The other must have been deleted. But under what conditions? We cannot simply say that a nucleus gets deleted when immediately preceded or followed by another nucleus, as we did in French. The imperfective forms show this to be incorrect. They start out with two nuclei and they end up with two nuclei. Why then do we lose a nucleus in the imperative forms and not in the imperfective forms? The answer is surprising: It is because of the tones. In the case of the imperfective form, we didn't lose any tones. We started out with a mid-high tone on the verb and another mid-high tone on the pronoun, and that's just how we finished. In the case of the imperative forms, the mid-high tone was lost. Suppose the presence of an associated tone prevents the loss of a nucleus in a sequence. In other words, we can say the following: In a nuclear sequence, delete any nucleus that has no associated tone. No nuclei fall under this condition in the imperfective forms. They all have associated tones. In the imperative form, however, the tone on the pronoun got lost. So its nucleus is now vulnerable and is deleted. Let me sum up the conditions on the three levels of structure and show how they indeed give us the results we seek.

(37) 1. *Segmental Level:* Delete a nonhigh vowel when immediately followed by another vowel.

    2. *Tonal Level:* Delete a mid-high tone when immediately preceded by a high tone.

    3. *Syllabic Level:* Delete any nucleus with no attached tone in a nuclear sequence.

Because we are dealing with three distinct levels of representation, a three dimensional rendition of this structure would be best. But we are limited to two dimensional paper, and so we have to imagine each level occupying its own plane. Let's now look at some derivations.

(38) pá + ò = [pó] 'throw him!'

Initial Representation

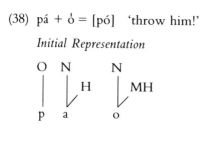

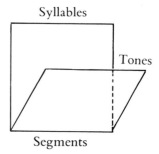

In (38), we see the three dimensional representation of the form *pá + ò*. The tones appear on the oblique lines heading off at an angle from the segments. The syllabic constituents are directly above the segments. In (38), we see that a nonhigh vowel, *a,* occurs immediately before another vowel and is deleted according to (37.1) to give us (39).

(39) O N   N
     | |
        H | MH
     | |/
     p   o

Notice that both the nucleus (N) and the high tone (H), formerly attached to the first vowel, are now floating. On the tonal tier, a mid-high tone immediately follows the high tone. This satisfies the condition of (37.2), and this tone is deleted, yielding (40).

(40) O N   N
     | |
        H |
     | |
     p   o

The floating high tone has an available vowel to which it can link, as in (41).

(41) O N   N
     | |
        H   /|
     | /
     p   o

However, the nucleus is not associated with any tone. (37.3) states it must go as well. This gives us the final form in (42).

(42)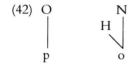

The overall picture is rather elegant, but there are some details that need attending to. In particular, the application of (37.3) is problematic. (37.3) states that nuclei with no attached tones are deleted. But in the representations that I have been using, tones are not attached directly to nuclei. Rather, both are linked to vowels. Once a vowel has been deleted, a tone cannot be linked to anything because direct tone–nucleus associations are not utilized in this representation. Thus, in example (40), neither nucleus has an attached tone, and perhaps both could undergo deletion. This is symptomatic of something lacking in our representations. But this is not the most serious problem.

Let's look at the form (36b), [jṵó] 'put her!'. This form is derived from the imperative verb *jú* followed by the third person object pronoun *ò*. *jú* contains a high vowel, thus there will be no deletion at the segmental level. Tonal deletion and nuclear deletion take place as before.

(43) jú + ò = [jṵó] 'put her!'

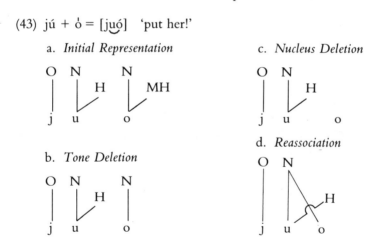

a. *Initial Representation*

c. *Nucleus Deletion*

b. *Tone Deletion*

d. *Reassociation*

In (43b), we see the results of tone deletion. The final nucleus is now toneless. A nucleus with no attached tone is subject to deletion, and this takes place in (43c). Now the final vowel, *o,* is floating. It seeks out the preceding nucleus and links to it, forming a diphthong. The representation still leaves something to be desired. The high tone is linked to the first vowel, *u,* although it is more clearly manifested on the second vowel, *o,* The diphthong sounds more or less like [wó], with the high vowel being realized more like a glide than a vowel. The length of this diphthong is the equivalent of a single vowel. That is, [wó] is not significantly longer than the [ó] of [pó]. The significance of this is seen shortly. Still, we see quite clearly how a diphthong is formed. After our deletions, we are left with two vowel segments and one syllabic position. In true autosegmental fashion, the floating vowel associates to the single nucleus, forming the segmental equivalent of a contour tone (two tones on one vowel).

It is the form of (36c) that reveals the major problem most clearly. This form consists of our high-voweled verb *jú* followed by another third person object pronoun, *ú*. The only difference between (36c) and (36b) is the vowel of the pronoun. The derivation should proceed exactly as in (43).

(44) jú + ú = [jú] 'put it!'

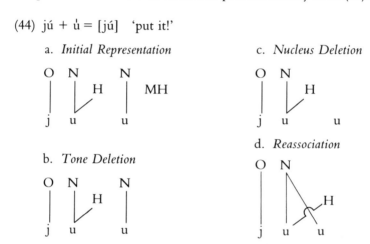

a. *Initial Representation*   c. *Nucleus Deletion*

b. *Tone Deletion*

d. *Reassociation*

Everything seems in order until we get to (44d). We wind up with two vowels attached to a single nucleus. In this case, both vowels are *u*. Recall that we had a similar situation with respect to tones. A vowel with two identical tones associated with it is no different than a vowel with a single tone. Logically, a nucleus should work the same way. The structures in (45) should, in theory, receive the same phonetic interpretation.

(45) a. N b. N

In both cases, the result should be [u]. Thus, (44d) should receive the interpretation [jú], and this is exactly right.

So, where is the problem? The problem is that we have no way of representing long vowels. Many languages, including English, make a distinction between long and short vowels. The English pair *beat–bit* gives some idea of what a vowel length distinction sounds like. The quality of the two vowels is not quite identical, but what interests us here is that the vowel of *beat* is significantly longer than that of *bit*. We allowed for such length distinctions in our syllable theory. Remember that any syllabic constituent may branch. This means that any syllabic constituent may contain up to two segments. A reasonable way to distinguish the nuclei of this English pair of words would be as follows:

(46) a. *The Nucleus of* bit   b. *The Nucleus of* beat

That is, the vowel of *beat* is roughly twice the length of that of *bit*. This length distinction is reflected by the branching nucleus in the former case. But the representation of (46b), which is supposed to represent a long vowel distinct from (46a), is formally identical to the representation of (45b), which is supposed to represent a short vowel identical to (45a). Furthermore, the diphthong in (43d) is no longer than a simple short vowel. The English diphthong [ay], as in *buy*, is significantly longer than a short vowel. In the present form of our representations, we would be obliged to represent the English word *buy* as follows:

(45) *English* buy

But now the long English diphthong in (47) has exactly the same representation as the short Dida diphthong in (43d). This won't do at all!

In this section we have seen that the assumption that segments are linked directly to syllabic constituents is fraught with difficulties. What we need is a level of structure that intervenes between the segments and the syllabic constituents. This level of structure is the subject of the next section.

The Skeleton

Suppose that we introduce another level of structure. The elements present at this level represent units of time. I use the symbol x to represent a timing unit. Of course, these timing units will have the same autosegmental properties as units found on other levels. Furthermore, they will be the pivot around which all the other levels turn. This means that tones, syllabic constituents, harmonic autosegments, and so on, will not be linked directly to segments but rather to these timing units. They, in turn, will be linked to the segments. This level of timing units is commonly called the *skeleton*. The units themselves are referred to as *points* or *positions*. The addition of the skeleton solves our representational problem. I will recast the Dida derivations, this time using a skeletal level. Notice also that the problem involving which nucleus to delete now disappears.

(48) *The Dida Analysis—with Skeleton*

    1. *Segmental Level:* Delete a nonhigh vowel when immediately followed by another vowel.

    2. *Tonal Level:* Delete a mid-high tone when immediately preceded by a high tone.

    3. *Skeleton:* Delete any nuclear point with no attached tone in a nuclear sequence.

(49) pá + ó = [pó] 'throw him!'

    a. *Initial Representation*

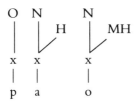

    b. *Vowel Deletion*

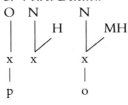

    c. *Tone Deletion*

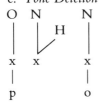

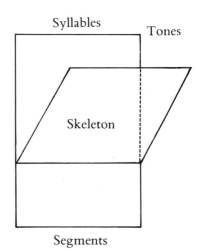

d. *Skeletal Point Deletion*   e. *Reassociation*

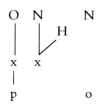   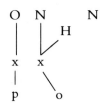

(50) jú + ŏ = [juǒ]   'put her!'

a. *Initial Representation*   c. *Skeletal Point Deletion*

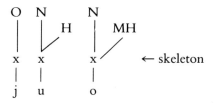

b. *Tone Deletion*   d. *Reassoication*

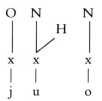   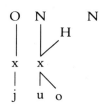

(51) jú + ǔ = [jú] 'put it!'

a. *Initial Representation*   c. *Skeletal Point Deletion*

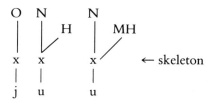   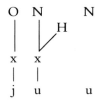

b. *Tone Deletion*   d. *Reassociation*

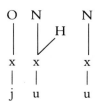

Derivations (49) to (51) are translations into skeletal terms of the forms that we consider earlier. I only considered (49) in detail. The other derivations should be straight forward. As before, the first nonhigh vowel is deleted (49b), and the mid–high tone has the same fate (49c). Notice that the skeletal position formerly occupied by *a* remains. The final point is not anchored by a tone, and so it is deleted also (49d). Now, both the final nucleus and the final vowel, *o,* are cut loose. The *o* finds a home at the unoccupied skeletal point. In the case of the floating nucleus we have two options, both of which will give the correct results. First, we can allow the nucleus to dock to the remaining point. This results in a single point with two associated nuclei. The normal autosegmental interpretation is to consider this configuration as identical to a point with a single nucleus, which is what we want. Or second, we could simply let the nucleus remain unattached. By convention, any unit not associated with a skeletal point receives no phonetic interpretation. Once more, the correct result is obtained. Notice that in this derivation the final form [pó] contains the nucleus, skeletal point, and tone of the stem syllable and the vowel of the suffix syllable.

In derivation (50) we solve the problem of the diphthong. The final form of this nucleus looks like this.

(52)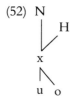

There are two segments associated to a single point. Skeletal points are timing units, therefore this configuration should be equivalent to a simple short vowel. This is indeed the case. The kind of diphthong shown in (52) can be called a *light* diphthong. It contains two vowel segments associated to a single skeletal position. The English long (or *heavy*) diphthongs can now receive a more perspicuous representation. They are longer than short vowels and so require two skeletal positions in their expression. The correct structure is given in (53).

(53)

The heavy diphthong in (53) contains two skeletal points, whereas the light diphthong of (51) only contains one. This reflects the fact that heavy diphthongs are significantly longer than short vowels. On the other hand, the light diphthong shown in (52) has a single point, giving it the same structure as a short vowel. This reflects the fact that light diphthongs are about the same length as short vowels.

What is worth noting in derivation (51) is that the final step yields a single skeletal point that has two identical vowels attached to it. This is what should be interpreted as the equivalent of a single short vowel. Because the skeletal point represents a timing unit, it should make no difference how many identical segments are attached to it. It can only take up the amount of time utilized by a single point. The problem concerning the representation of long vowels is also solved. As their name suggests, long vowels are longer than short vowels. The logic of our theory tells us that they must have an additional timing unit. The representation of a long vowel is shown in (54).

(54)

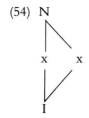

(54) could represent the long vowel of *beat*. Notice that it has the same structure as the heavy diphthong in (53). The only difference is that a long vowel has a single unit on the segmental tier, whereas a heavy diphthong has two such units.

The analytic part of this translation is shown in (48). What has changed from the nonskeletal version is that now we delete a skeletal point, rather than a nucleus, when no tone anchors it. This is conceptually simpler because tones actually are anchored to skeletal points and not directly to nuclei. It also provides an amusing possibility to test another aspect of autosegmental theory. Recall the discussion of tonal representations. In that section, I advanced the hypothesis that a mid tone was simply the realization of the absence of tone on a vowel. We now have another way of testing this hypothesis. The Dida analysis presented earlier makes crucial reference to the presence of a tone on the tonal tier. In a nuclear sequence, a skeletal point with no associated tone is dropped. If a mid tone is really the absence of tone, we would expect to lose a position each time a verb with a mid tone is followed by an object pronoun. Remember that no points were lost in the case of imperfective verbs having a mid-high tone. The expression *pá* + *ó* 'throws him' yielded [póó]. No tone or position was lost, only the first vowel segment. The derivation follows:

(55)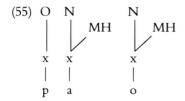

Note that each nuclear position is accompanied by a tone. The initial nonhigh vowel of the sequence is deleted, but its position remains.

(56)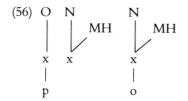

The remaining vowel, *o*, spreads to the now vacant position.

(57)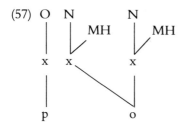

Now, the *o* occupies both nuclear positions. Each of these positions has an associated mid-high tone. Thus, (57) does indeed represent [póó].

With this example in mind, let's replace the mid-high verb *pá* 'throws' by a verb with a mid tone: *la* 'carries'. We want to derive the form 'carries him', which should start out as *la* plus *ó*.

(58) 1a + o' 'carries him'
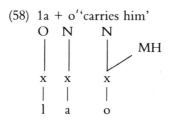

The structure in (58) is identical to that of (55) except that the first nuclear point has no tone here. On the segmental level, the first of the two vowels is nonhigh, and so it is deleted.[15]

(59)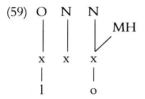

The first nucleus is not protected by an associated tone, and so it too should fall.

(60)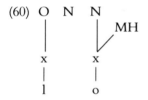

As discussed earlier we need not worry about the floating nucleus. It will have no effect on the interpretation of this structure. What we have left is an onset position containing the segment *l* followed by a nuclear position carrying a mid-high tone and the segment *o*. If our analysis is correct, the Dida form 'carries him' should be pronounced [ló], and it is!

The introduction of a skeleton allows us to provide a simple account of the phenomena just discussed. We have an intuitively satisfying representation for such things as light and heavy diphthongs as well as long and short vowels. The skeleton is the intersection at which the other levels meet. More and more processes can be described by our putting things together–pulling things apart formula. This theory is much more restrictive than the SPE rule-based theory. We immediately see the connection between the process and the context in which it occurs. For example, in our so-called assimilation cases, we are really only deleting a vowel and spreading a neighboring vowel to the vacated position. We can now return to our discussion of French devocalization and proceed with the solution of the mysteries surrounding this process.

You recall that in French a high vowel was realized as a corresponding

---

[15]There is no particular reason to treat the segmental level before the skeletal level, as I have done here. I could just as well have gotten rid of the skeletal point before deleting the vowel segment.

glide when immediately followed by another vowel. We showed this to be a case of moving a segment from a nuclear position to an onset position. This analysis was presented in preskeletal terms, but nothing much changes with the addition of this additional level. The hypothesis of a syllabic basis for this process was reinforced by the fact that it could not occur before saturated onsets, that is, onsets already containing two segments. Recall further that any phonetic explanation of this phenomenon was rejected because of the existence of consonant–liquid–glide sequences. For convenience, I repeat the examples in (61).

(61) *French Consonant–Liquid–Glide Sequences*

trois	'three'	[trwa]	pluie	'rain'	[plẅi]
emploi	'job'	[āplwa]	truite	'trout'	[trẅit]
croix	'cross'	[krwa]	bruit	'noise'	[brẅi]

If our syllable theory is correct, this sequence cannot fit into an onset. All syllabic constituents are limited to a maximum of two positions. With the introduction of the skeleton, a new way of analyzing these forms is made possible. While looking at the Dida examples, we learned about the existence of light diphthongs. These diphthongs consist of a high vowel followed by another vowel, both of which are associated to a single point. In (61), I have transcribed the French examples with a glide rather than a high vowel, but this is misleading. We have also learned that glides and high vowels are really the same thing; only their syllabic position distinguishes them. Now, it is possible to take a phonetic form such as [trwa] and fit it into a well-formed (as defined by our theory) syllable structure. It will look like (62). (I have continued my practice of writing an uppercase letter to represent a segment that is indifferently a high vowel or a glide.)

(62)

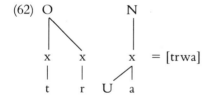

In (62), we see a branching onset containing two segments: *t* and *r*. This is certainly a possible onset. The following nucleus contains a single point with two segments attached to it. This is a light diphthong, the structural equivalent to a short vowel. This too is permitted by our theory of syllable structure. Thus, it appears we can explain, on the one hand, why no devocalization takes place in a form such as *plier,* and on the other, how it is that we can find consonant–liquid–glide clusters in forms such as *trois* [trwa]. The skeleton provides the answer.

In the case of *plier,* there is one point too many. Let's reconsider its derivation.

(63)

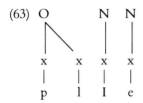

We have already noted that French does not like sequences of successive nuclei.[16] As before, the first nucleus of the sequence is deleted.

(64)

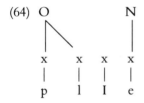

We must now find a home for the orphaned point, along with its segment *I.* We cannot put it into the onset, because this latter constituent is already saturated with its two positions. Why not put it in the nucleus? This would yield the following structure:

(65)

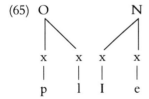

What is important to note here is that we have *not* formed a light diphthong in (65). The branching nuclear structure represents a heavy diphthong. This is not at all the same structure as that proposed for [trwa]. There, a single nuclear point was associated with two vowel segments. If the nucleus of (65) is a heavy and not a light diphthong, why not just form a

---

[16]Unlike Dida and Vata, which tolerate them. This is apparently a parameter along which linguistic systems may differ. The Dida and Vata cases involved deletion of vowels and sometimes points, but not nuclei.

heavy diphthong and have done with it? In fact, there are a number of possible answers to this question. I'll just use the simplest. Any theory of syllable structure must answer the following question: What is a possible heavy diphthong? One could imagine a theory in which *any* two vowel segments associated to the two points of a branching nucleus would be a possible heavy diphthong. It turns out that this is not the case. Heavy diphthongs have a very definite ordering with respect to their segments. Specifically, a heavy diphthong begins with a vowel and ends with a glide. In our terms, this means that a heavy diphthong must end in a high vowel (i.e., something that could be interpreted as a glide). This is not what we see in (65). There, the branching nucleus begins with a high vowel rather than ending with one. It is not a possible heavy diphthong, and so the structure of (65) is ill formed at the segmental level. You will notice that English heavy diphthongs, which are exceedingly common, invariably end with a glide: *boy, buy, cow,* and so on. In any event, the structure in (65) is not a possible foster home for our orphaned point. This notion of possible heavy diphthong may sound quite ad hoc as I have presented it. A more technical discussion, which would take us beyond the scope of this book, would show that it follows from very general, well-established principles of phonological theory.

We must conclude then that there is no haven for the unsyllabified point in (64). It cannot link to the onset, nor can it link to the nucleus. The result is that we cannot delete a nucleus in (63). To do so leads us to the current predicament. So the nucleus stays. This still leaves us with a sequence of nuclei—something that French doesn't like at all. What if we were to break up this sequence, say, by inserting a constituent between the two nuclei? Let's think about syllable structure. Syllabic constituents generally come in pairs: an onset and a rime (which I have simplified to a nucleus in this discussion). One way of thinking of syllable structure is to assume that this pair-wise relation is always present, at least potentially. In other words, the level of syllable structure contains the sequence *O N* repeated sufficiently to take care of the points and segments in the given form. If this virtual or implicit onset that separates the two offending nuclei can be realized, that is, can be identified by its association with some segment, we have found a way out of our problem. The resulting structure at the syllable level would then be *O N O N,* which is fine, rather than *O N N,* which is not.

Suppose we begin with (66).

(66)

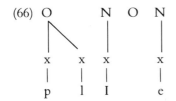

Here, we have a floating onset between the two nuclei. It is not attached to a point, thus for all intents and purposes it is invisible (and certainly inaudible). The two nuclei can see each other and they don't like what they see. Getting rid of one of them does not help, as we have seen. What if we could make the invisible onset visible? We could do this by associating some segmental material to it, in which case it would no longer float and would thus break up the nuclear sequence. What we need is a segment that could associate to an onset. But remember, we cannot allow any association lines to cross. This eliminates both *p* and *l* because they would have to cross *l*'s association line in order to get at the available onset. The obvious candidate is *I* itself. Remember that high vowels and glides are segmentally identical. When attached to a nuclear point they are realized as vowels. When linked to an onset position they come out as glides. It follows then that *I* can link either to a nucleus or an onset, or both!

(67)

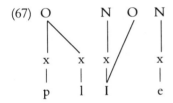

One thing is funny about the representation in (67): We have a segment directly linked to a syllabic constituent *with no intervening skeletal point*. There is no way of interpreting such a structure. What we need to do is add a convention for turning a structure like (67) into something we can interpret. Here is the convention:

(68) Let Σ be any syllabic constituent, and σ, any segment, then the structure

must be interpreted as

In other words, any time we find a segment linked directly to a syllabic constituent, we add a skeletal point. This may seem to be a bit of a fudging, but it's the best we can do for the moment. In any event, there is never any need to distinguish the two structures in (68), so we might as well say they are the same. If we apply (68) to (67) we get (69).

(69)

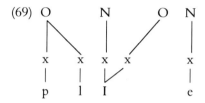

Now we *can* interpret this structure. It consists of two syllables. The first syllable contains a branching onset *pl* followed by a simple nucleus *I*. A nuclear *I* is [i], and so the entire first syllable is [pli]. The second syllable contains an onset *I* followed by a simple nucleus *e*. A nonnuclear *I* is pronounced [y], and so the second syllable is pronounced [ye]. Putting things together gives us [pliye], which is, lo and behold, exactly the pronunciation of *plier*. Now we know where the mysterious glide came from. It is nothing more than the preceding vowel spread onto the onset position. This latter position is now properly identified—it is linked to a segment—and our nuclear sequence no longer exists. This is quite a lovely result. In similar fashion, we can derive the remaining forms of (27), [truwe] and [glüw̃ā]. The glides that separate the two vowels are nothing more than the nonnuclear manifestations of the preceding vowels.

One final bit of business needs to be taken care of. We escaped from the problem of the occurring consonant—liquid—glide sequences by saying that these were light diphthongs, found in the nucleus. This saved us from having to posit onsets with three segments and losing our entire explanation for the failure of devocalization to apply in forms such as *plier, trouer,* and *gluant.* It's easy to say that the sequence [wa] in [trwa] *trois* is a light diphthong. But can we prove it? Failure to do so would leave us open to the accusation of playing fast and loose with syllable structure in order to get ourselves out of the consonant—liquid—glide problem.

Let's look at the sequence [wa] more closely. There are at least two possible syllabic interpretations that it can receive in French. There is the light diphthong interpretation that we have posited for *trois.* In that case, *U* shares a nuclear point with the vowel *a.* But *U* can equally be linked to an onset, which in turn would be followed by a simple nucleus containing just *a.* Both structures are given in (70).

(70) a. *Light Diphthong*   b. *Onset–Nucleus*

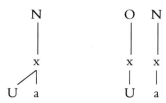

I am assuming that these two structures receive an identical phonetic interpretation. They are both pronounced [wa]. This means that there is no way to tell what the syllable structure of the sequence [wa] is just by listening to it. If we want to show that the light diphthong in French exists, we need a way of determining its syllable structure. Fortunately, French provides us with a solution. In many contexts, there are processes in French that are sensitive to syllable structure. Specifically, they are sensitive to words that begin with vowels (or, more exactly, words whose first segment is found in the nucleus) versus words that have a segment in the onset position. The following examples illustrate this sensitivity:

(71) le mur   'the wall'   [lë mür]   l'ami   'the friend'   [lami]
     les murs 'the walls' [le mür]   les amis 'the friends' [lezami]
     ce mur   'this wall' [së mür]   cet ami 'this friend' [sɛtami]

In (71), I compare two nouns: one (*mur*) beginning with a consonant and one (*ami*) beginning with a vowel. The latter example must begin with the structure of (70a), without the second segment attached to the nucleus. The consonant-initial example should have the syllable structure shown in (70b). What is important is that in one case there is a nonempty onset and in the other case the onset has no segmental content. I have presented three processes that are sensitive to this contrast. First, the vowel of the definite article is elided before a vowel-initial word (cf. *l'ami* not *le ami*). Second, the plural suffix -*s* is attached to a following vowel-initial word. This does not happen to words beginning with consonants (cf. [lezami] not *[le ami], [le mü] not *[lezmür]). Finally, the form of the masculine demonstrative article is *ce* before words beginning with consonants and *cet* before words beginning with vowels. At least at the beginnings of words we should have no difficulty in deciding whether we are dealing with a structure like (70a) or (70b). If French really does have light diphthongs as in (70a), then the sequence [wa] should be ambiguous. We predict that certain French words beginning with [wa] should behave like *ami* (i.e., those with a light diphthong), whereas others should behave like *mur* (i.e., those with an onset-nucleus analysis). This remarkable prediction is absolutely true.

(72) [wat]   'watt'   [wazo]   'bird'
     [lë wat] 'the watt'   [lwazo]   'the bird'
     [le wat] 'the watts'   [lezwazo]   'the birds'
     [cë wat] 'this watt'   [cɛtwazo]   'this bird'

The noun for 'watt' consistently displays behavior associated with a consonant-initial word: There is no truncation, the plural suffix is not pronounced, and the form of the demonstrative article is *ce*. On the other hand, 'bird' behaves just like a vowel-initial word: The vowel of the article is elided, we hear the plural suffix, and the form of the demonstrative article is *cet*. We shouldn't be fooled by the way these two words are spelled in French. [wazo] is spelled *oiseau* and [wat] is spelled *watt*. The pronunciation of the sequence [wa] is identical for both words. The French spelling certainly reflects the difference in syllable structure, but it is not the cause of this difference.

The ultimate example of this kind of syllabic ambiguity is a single word that can go either way, depending on the whim of the speaker. That is, some speakers treat this word as beginning with a light diphthong, others do not. The word is [wat], spelled *ouate* and meaning 'wad' or 'padding', as in *a wad of cotton*. This word is a homonym of *watt* but differs in gender (it is feminine). All the forms given in (73) are possible.

(73) [la wat]   [lwat]   'the wad'
     [le wat]   [lezwat]   'the wads'
     [ma wat]   [mõnwat]   'my wad'[17]

This example shows convincingly that syllable structure is not directly tied to raw pronunciation. French speakers who treat [wat] as diphthong-initial do not pronounce this word any differently than those who treat it as onset-initial. Furthermore, once a choice has been made, speakers are absolutely consistent. Anyone who says [la wat] must also say [le wat]. The form [lezwat] is impossible. The reverse case is equally true. Someone who says [lwat] cannot say [le wat]. Only [lezwat] is possible for such a speaker.

In this section, we have seen how syllable structure and the skeleton allow us to explain a wide variety of phenomena. What is encouraging is that the analysis of phonological processes is becoming progressively simpler and less arbitrary. The same sorts of governing principles crop up again and again. We see that tones, harmonic features, syllabic constituents, and skeletal points all behave in much the same way. One class of phonological phenomena remains to be discussed. Indeed, one of the major objectives of

---

[17]The form of the first person feminine possessive pronoun is *ma* before consonants and *mon* before vowels. Cf. *ma fille* 'my girl' vs. *mon amie* 'my girl friend'.

SPE was to provide a reasonable account of these processes. I am referring to accentual phenomena.

METRICAL PHONOLOGY;
THE TAMING OF STRESS

When phonologists talk about stress they are not referring to our internal reaction to traffic jams, job interviews, exam taking, or the like. In polysyllabic words (those with more than one syllable), one syllable is always produced in a more prominent fashion than the others. Certain aspects of English stress were discussed in chapter 3. It happens that English has one of the most complex stress systems encountered till now. Providing a reasonable analysis for this phenomenon has been the subject of many books. Over 100 pages of SPE were devoted to this subject. I certainly do not go through all the details and intricacies of this problem. As far as English stress is concerned, coming up with any analysis is a considerable achievement. To give you a small taste of what some early results looked like, I present in (74) the final version of the English main stress rule (yes, it was not the only rule) taken from SPE (Chomsky & Halle, 1968, p. 240).

(74)

MAIN STRESS

$$V \rightarrow [1 \text{ stress}] \Big/ \left[X\text{---}C_0 \left(\begin{bmatrix} -\text{tense} \\ \gamma\text{stress} \\ V \end{bmatrix} C_0^\prime \left(\begin{bmatrix} \alpha\text{voc} \\ \alpha\text{cons} \\ -\text{ant} \end{bmatrix} \right) \right) \right.$$

$$\left(\left\{ \begin{matrix} (fik)At \\ [+D]C_0 \end{matrix} \right\} \right) \left\{ \begin{matrix} \langle_1 + C_0 \rangle_1 \begin{bmatrix} -\text{stress} \\ -\text{tense} \\ -\text{cons} \end{bmatrix} [+\text{cons}]_0 \\ \langle_1 \begin{bmatrix} -\text{seg} \\ \langle_2-\text{FB}\rangle_2 \end{bmatrix} \rangle_1 C_0 [\beta\text{stress}]C_0 \langle_2 V_0 C_0 \rangle_2 \end{matrix} \right\} \langle \text{NSP}\langle_1 VA\rangle_1 \rangle$$

Conditions: $\beta = \left\{ \begin{matrix} 2 \\ 1 \end{matrix} \right\}$

$\gamma \le 2$

X contains no internal #

This is a fairly discouraging result! If (74) is a possible stress rule, then what isn't? It should come as no surprise that many phonologists, including one of the authors of SPE, have spent considerable time and energy searching for a more believable account for stress systems in general and English stress in particular.[18] The breakthrough came in the middle of the 1970s. In

---

[18]For example, Halle and Vergnaud (1987).

a seminal article, Liberman and Prince (1977) showed that stress, like so many other phonological phenomena, was best treated with a nonlinear approach. Rules were deemed inappropriate descriptive devices for such phenomena. One look at rule (74) is enough to convince anyone that they were right. They proposed an additional level of structure intermediate between segments and words. Syllables, or more precisely rimes, were organized at this level. Because many of the ideas and terminology stemmed from the study of poetic meter, this approach was dubbed *metrical phonology*.

In order to better understand the inner workings of this theory, I present one relatively simple stress system and show what a metrical analysis would look like. The example comes to us from Ojibwa, a Canadian Indian language spoken in Ontario. In the following examples, stress is indicated, as before, with an acute accent. Long vowels are written with a following colon (:).

(75) masína'íkán   'book'   ni-másiná'ikán   'my book'
      namátapí   'he sits'   ni-námatáp   'I sit'
      namátapí-wák   'they sit'
      wí:ssiní   'he eats'   ni-wí:ssín   'I eat'
      wí:ssiní-wák   'they eat'
      akkwé:sé:ns   'girl'   nit-ákkwé:sé:ns-ím 'my girl'

The position of stress in Ojibwa is completely predictable. This means that given any phonological string, we can formulate an algorithm that will allow us to assign stress to the appropriate syllables. Here is the algorithm:

(76) 1. All long vowels are stressed.
      2. All final syllables are stressed.
      3. Starting from a long vowel or the beginning of a word, stress all the even numbered syllables.

For example, consider the form *masina'ikan*. Let's apply (76) to this form. To facilitate this task, I number the syllables.

(77)   1 2   3 4   5
       m a s i n a ' i k a n

There are no long vowels in this form, so (76.1) does not apply. (76.2) does, and we can stress the final syllable.

(78)   1 2   3 4   5
       m a s i n a ' i k á n

It remains now to stress the even numbered syllables starting from the beginning of the word (there are no long vowels). Thus, syllables 2 and 4 are stressed.

(79)   1 2 3 4 5
        m a s í n a ' í k á n

The form in (79) corresponds to the desired output. Let's look at a form with a long vowel.

(80)   1   2   3
        w i: ss i n i w a k

The form in (80) does contain a long vowel, which is stressed by (76.1). (76.2) will cause the final vowel to be stressed, yielding (81).

(81)   1   2   3
        w í: ss i n i w á k

Now, we start counting syllables. The first syllable is a long vowel, thus we start our count on the following syllable. Syllable 2 will receive stress by (76.3).

(82)   1   2   3
        w í: ss i n í w á k

Once again, we have derived the correct form.

Applying this algorithm to the remaining forms of (75) will yield the correct result in all cases. We can, of course, propose some rules that will generate all these forms.

(83) a. $[+\text{syll}] \rightarrow [+\text{stress}] / \underline{\hspace{1cm}}(C)\#$

 b. $\begin{bmatrix} +\text{syll} \\ +\text{long} \end{bmatrix} \rightarrow [+\text{stress}]$

 c. $[+\text{syll}] \rightarrow [+\text{stress}] / [-\text{stress}] \, C_0 \underline{\hspace{1cm}}$

Rule (83a) says that any final vowel is stressed. The parenthesized C allows for the possibility of a final consonant. All long vowels are stressed according to rule (83b). Finally, (83c) stresses any vowel that follows an unstressed vowel. The expression C_0 is matched by any number of consonants or the null string (i.e., no consonants). It is (83c) that gives us the alternating effect. It is crucial that (83c) apply after (83b) and that it apply in an iterative fashion going from left to right. I pick up the derivation following the application of rules (83a and 83b).

(84)   1 2 3 4 5
        m a s i n a ' i k á n

(83c) cannot apply to syllable 1 because it is not preceded by a stressless vowel. Moving to the next syllable to the right, we see that the context for (83c) is satisfied. Syllable 2 is preceded by a stressless syllable, and so the rule applies, yielding (85).

(85)   1 2 3 4 5
        m a s í n a ' i k á n

Continuing to scan the string from left to right, we see that syllable 3 is now immediately preceded by a [+stress] vowel. We skip to syllable 4, and once more the rule can apply because syllable 3 is [−stress] (the default value of this feature). Reapplying rule (83c) derives the final form.

(86)   1 2 3 4 5
        m a s í n a ' í ká n

   The rules of (83) suffer from the same problem that afflicts any SPE–type rule. They treat the entire Ojibwa stress system as something quite arbitrary. This objection can be made for any phonological analysis based on rules. There is one major problem specific to the rule in (83), namely rules (83a) and (83c) are considered to be autonomous objects. In the rule–based approach, there is no logical connection between the rule that stresses final syllables and the one that stresses a vowel following a stressless vowel. One could easily imagine a system containing one without the other. The problem is that in real life, no system can have rule (83c) without having rule (83a) as well. It is a mistake to consider the two as independent events. Any successful account of these stress facts must find a way of relating these two phenomena. Metrical phonology provides such an account.
   Metrical phonology recognizes a constituent that is greater than a syllable and less than a word.[19] In fact, this constituent is composed of syllables, or more exactly, parts of syllables. It is called a *metrical foot* (or simply a foot). Feet are groupings of syllables and are of two types: binary feet, which have at most two members, and unbounded feet, which may contain an indefinitely large number of members. It is the former type that is of interest here. Each foot consists of a strong member and zero or more weak members. If a foot has only one member, it is strong. Binary feet will have one strong and

---

[19]A detailed account of metrical theory can be found in Hayes (1980).

one weak member. Unbounded feet will contain one strong member. All the other members are weak. There are only two positions in a foot where a strong member can be found: at the beginning or at the end. Strong members are always found at foot edges.

Languages may vary as to whether feet are left–dominant (the strong member is found at the beginning) or right–dominant (the strong member is found at the end). Languages may also impose constraints on what type of rime can occur in a weak position. In some languages, any rime may occur in weak positions. In other languages, rimes with more than one position (i.e., branching nuclei or branching rimes) are excluded from such positions. We also have a choice of which direction our foot construction takes place in. We can construct feet starting from the left or the right edge of a word. Stress systems can then be defined in terms of a small number of parameters along which one system can vary from another. This is an example of the parametric approach discussed in an earlier chapter. The Ojibwa stress system can now be defined as follows:

(87) Starting from the left edge of a word, construct binary right–dominant feet. Branching nuclei (i.e., long vowels) may not occupy a weak position.

I apply this recipe to the Ojibwa examples. I use the symbol F to represent a foot, s for a strong member, and w for a weak member.

(88) a. *Initial Form*   m a s i n a ' i k a n
      b. *Foot Construction*

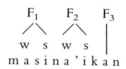

$$
\begin{array}{ccc}
F_1 & F_2 & F_3 \\
\diagup\diagdown & \diagup\diagdown & | \\
w \quad s & w \quad s & \\
\end{array}
$$
m a s i n a ' i k a n

Foot construction has taken place from left to right. The first two vowels, *a* and *i*, have been gathered into a right–dominant binary foot. Thus, *a* is the weak member and *i* is the strong member of F_1. Continuing to the right, we can group the next two vowels into another foot, F_2. A single syllable remains, and so it forms a degenerate foot—a foot consisting of a single vowel. Stress assignment is now quite straight forward: Simply assign a stress to the strong member of each foot. Applying this to the metrical structure in (88) yields the correct output.

(89)
$$
\begin{array}{ccc}
F_1 & F_2 & F_3 \\
\diagup\diagdown & \diagup\diagdown & | \\
w \quad s & w \quad s & \\
\end{array}
$$
m a s ɪ n a ' i k á n

Remember that as a degenerate foot, F_3 contains only a strong member. Thus, a vowel of a generage foot is always stressed.

Let's now consider a form with a long vowel.

(90) a. *Initial Form*   w i: ss i n i w a k
     b. *Foot Construction*

The initial vowel of this form is long. The Ojibwa system excludes long vowels from occupying weak positions in feet. Therefore, we must construct a degenerate foot on the first syllable. The second syllable cannot be incorporated into this foot because feet are right-dominant. If we included the second syllable, it would be the strong member of the foot and the first syllable would be the weak member. But long vowels cannot occupy weak positions, and so a binary foot with an initial long vowel is impossible. The second and third syllables can be grouped together to form F_2. A final syllable remains, and it forms another degenerate foot. Stressing the strong members of feet once again yields the correct result.

(91) F_1 F_2 F_3
     | /\ |
     | w s |
     w í: ss i n í w á k

These procedures make it possible to derive all the examples presented in (75); indeed it is possible to assign stress correctly to every Ojibwa word. Because long vowels cannot occupy weak positions they must always carry stress. Either they are found in the right position of a foot, which is the strong position and hence stress bearing, or else they form a degenerate foot and so will bear stress as the only member of the foot. The fact that feet are right-dominant and that foot construction proceeds from left to right also guarantees that every final syllable will be stressed. The final syllable will either be the right member of a foot and accordingly stressed or else it will be the odd one out and form a degenerate foot, in which case it will also be stressed. The fact that all final syllables are stressed is no longer a separate phenomenon in metrical phonology. It is simply an automatic consequence of how feet are constructed.

The binary nature of these feet accounts for the use of terms *odd* and *even* in earlier frameworks. It is difficult to imagine a speaker of Ojibwa calculating in advance if the syllable about to be pronounced is an odd or even number of syllables away from the word edge or the nearest long vowel and assigning the stress accordingly. Constructing binary feet offers a conceptually appealing way of thinking about how such systems operate.

An even more impressive achievement of metrical phonology is that now stress systems can be defined in terms of a very small number of parameters (around 10). This parameterization of at least one subsystem of phonology takes us toward our ultimate goal of defining a possible phonological system. Stress is no longer the formal nightmare that created such monstrosities as rule (74). It can now be defined as a core system embodying foot construct routines that is fleshed out by fixing the parameters appropriate to the specific stress system in question.

In this chapter, we have seen that the autosegmental approach, which has enjoyed such success in the analysis of tonal systems, can be usefully applied to a broad range of nontonal phenomena. Harmonic systems share much in common with tonal ones and it is normal that they be subject to the same theoretical restrictions. We have seen that syllable structure plays a major role in the analysis of certain processes. This structure is abstract in the sense that it cannot always be read off directly from the signal. Nevertheless, the evidence for its presence in phonological representation is quite convincing. Syllable constituents also display the types of autosegmental properties found in other phonological subsystems. In addition, the postulation of a skeletal level of representation allows us to account for a rich variety of facts using this same restricted theory of phonological processes. What must be treated as arbitrary or accidental in a rule-based approach can now be explained using general principles whose scope extends far beyond the phenomenon in question.

Phonology has come a long way in 20 years. In the next and final chapter, I discuss the frontiers of current phonological research. The nature of phonological representations has changed drastically from the days of SPE. The latest theoretical advances have significant implications in such areas as speech parsing and automatic speech recognition. As the nature of phonological representations and processes becomes clearer, there is more temptation to speculate on why things are the way they are. Once more, I succumb to this temptation.

5

Current Phonological Research and Its Implications

The image of phonological representations has changed greatly in the last 20 years. We have a multitude of different levels with a latticework of connecting association lines. At the center of all this is the skeleton, a series of timing units. Events take place at a given level with the other tiers remaining unchanged. The effects of these events are seen in the new associations created between the various levels. It may appear that phonological representations have grown more complex, but this is open to question. As each level is added, more and more phonological phenomena have become amenable to an autosegmental treatment. The relationship between a phonological event and the context in which it occurs is no longer an arbitrary one. Phonological events are *local*. An element on a given level may spread to a neighboring unit. Deletion may take place subject to local conditions. Reassociation involves reattachment of association lines to the nearest available position, and so on. The organizing principles of the various levels bear a strong resemblance to one another. Current phonological research involves the search for this set of general principles. Systemic variation, how one phonological system may differ from another, can be reduced to a series of parameters. Elements may spread to the left or to the right; sequences of identical elements are eliminated by deleting the left member or the right member, or by interposing another element; syllable systems may contain branching rimes or they may not; and so on.

Parameterized systems enjoy an important advantage over rule-based ones: The former are closed systems, whereas the latter are essentially open. Parameterized systems may vary along very limited and well-defined axes. They involve a series of (usually binary) decisions, and each choice results in a possible phonological system. The idea is that a parameterized theory has just enough expressive power to encompass the set of possible phonological systems. Phenomena that are deemed to be impossible are, ideally, inexpressible in parameterized theories.

Rule-based systems are open in the sense that they impose no limit on what a possible phonological process can be. Even the simplest phonological rule implicitly implies an impressive number of choices. The specification of any feature figuring in the rule might be changed, different features might replace those occurring, features might be added or subtracted from the original process. The result is almost always nonsensical. Rule-based theories do not give us a clear idea of what a possible phonological process is. It follows that they offer little hope of explaining the existence of phonology or why it has the particular form that it does. Finally, a rule-based theory gives little insight into possible applications of phonology such as parsing, learning theory, and automatic speech recognition.

Consider the case of phonological parsing. We have seen that a morpheme with a single lexical representation may occur in a variety of phonetic realizations due to the action of various phonological processes. It is reasonable to assume that speakers do not store every phonetic form. These forms are by and large predictable once we know what the phonological processes are. The parsing problem is then to take a phonetic input and match it against the list of lexical representations stored in the brain. In order to do this, the effect of the phonological processes must be undone. That is, we must perform the converse of a phonological derivation. Starting with a phonetic form, we must deduce its source. What underlying form could have led to the production of this form? In the early 1970s, such parsers were constructed.[1] The results were quite startling. Even with full knowledge of all the phonological processes involved, the program churned out hundreds of possible sources for relatively simple input forms. This is hardly a plausible model for human linguistic behavior. The idea of performing hundreds, or even tens, of matching operations on each input morpheme in order to successfully identify it is difficult to swallow. Experience with parser construction does permit us to identify the nature of the

---

[1] Phillips (1971) is one example. Her parser was based on a phonological calculator that applied rules to underlying forms in order to derive phonetic output (see Kaye & Roosen-Runge, 1973).

problem. The success of a parser in reducing the number of possible sources for a given form varies inversely with the openness of our system. A phonological theory, such as a rule-based one, that says that nearly anything can be a phonological process or a phonological derivation offers little help to a parser seeking the source for an input form. To the extent that phonological theory narrows the scope of possibilities, the work of the parser is facilitated. Indeed, the period of interest in building phonological calculators and parsers petered out rapidly early in the 1970s. Rule-based systems were simply not computationally very interesting.

If the parsing problem proved difficult for rule-based systems, the learning problem was an absolute nightmare. Machine learning of phonological systems involves presenting the machine with a series of input forms, in much the same way that a child receives linguistic input, and attempting to construct the phonology based on these data. Once more, the difficulty of the task increases with the openness of the system. It is much easier to set a switch than to select a member of an indefinitely large set. It is amusing to contemplate a scenario leading to the acquisition of the English main stress rule as it is expressed in the previous chapter. It is not surprising then that as phonological theory became more and more restrictive, the interest in its computational properties, dormant for several years, has been rekindled. Parameterized systems are much more interesting from the point of view of parser construction, learning models, and automatic speech recognition.[2] Given the current interest in areas such as artificial intelligence, expert systems, and natural language interfaces, it can now be said that phonological theory is rapidly approaching the stage where it can be profitably applied to these areas. This potential is certainly not limited to phonology. Similar results in syntactic theory have similar consequences. We are witnessing the birth of a true applied linguistics.

On a more theoretical note, current phonological theory provides an interesting answer to one of our earliest questions: What is the ultimate phonological unit? Classical generative phonology maintained the segment defined as a matrix of features as its ultimate unit. This was fully in keeping with the notion of the *phoneme,* the heritage of classical generative phonology's immediate predecessor: structural linguistics. The assumption was that there exists a list of entities that make up the phonemic inventory of a given language. These entities could be considered atomic, as in many versions of structural linguistics, or as bundles of features, as in generative phonology. In the following section, we see that current advances in phonological theory pose serious problems for notion of the phoneme.

---

[2]A computational model for the acquisition of stress systems has been constructed. See Dresher and Kaye (in press) for details.

THE DEATH OF THE PHONEME

Back in the 1940s, phonologists spent a lot of time and ink on the discussions of the nature and definition of the ultimate phonological unit. The idea of a segment, which they called a phoneme, seemed intuitively satisfying. It corresponded to many, but by no means all, of the writing systems of the world's languages. Certain sounds were present in some languages but not in others. It was natural to compare languages by comparing their phonological inventories: the list of consonant and vowels employed by each language. Segments changed into other segments. Entire segments were lost through deletion processes or created through epenthesis. What could be more natural than a phonological segment? The image of such entities had pervaded phonological thinking for decades, if not centuries. The consequence of current phonological research is unequivocal: The phoneme now enjoys the same status in phonology as does the ether in physics. It is an illusion.

Let me ask a very simple question: How many vowels are there in Latin? Or, more precisely, how many vowel segments (phonemes) are there in Latin? In school, we may have learned that Latin has 10 vowels: 5 short vowels and 5 long vowels. In Latin texts, vowel length was not distinguished, but in grammars a horizontal line, called a macron, was placed over a vowel to indicate that it was long. I use a colon to indicate vowel length in this discussion. Latin may be said to have the following vowel system:

(1) *The Latin Vowel System*

Short Vowels		Long Vowels	
i	u	i:	u:
e	o	e:	o:
a		a:	

Each of these vowels can be shown to contrast with the nine others. That is, we can find pairs of words whose only difference is in having one vowel rather than another. These *minimal pairs* were an essential tool of structural linguistics and led to the postulation of a 10-vowel system for Latin. The methodology of classical generative phonology differed in important respects from structural linguistics, but the results were the same: Latin had a 10-vowel system. One could use the feature [long] to distinguish the long vowels from the short ones. One proposed 10 feature matrices to define the 10 vowel phonemes.

Today, the answer is not so clear. Does Latin have 10 vowel phonemes?

Let's look at how they are represented in modern theory. For the moment, let's suppose that the segmental level of representation contains feature matrices à la SPE. I will continue to use alphabetic symbols to represent these feature bundles. Consider the representation of a short *a* versus a long *a:*.

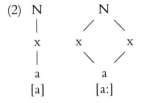

(2)

It is not so clear whether or not *a* and *a:* represent two separate phonemes. On the segmental level they are identical. In fact, they are different only in their syllable structure. Phonemes are not traditionally distinguished by their position in syllable structure. For example, an *s* appearing in the onset position is considered to be the same segment as an *s* occurring in the rime. The structures in (3) are not supposed to represent two different phonemes.

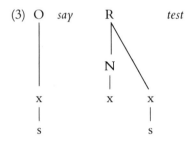

(3)   O   *say*   R   *test*

Nor is it the case that any sequence exclusively contained within a syllabic constituent is considered a phoneme. For example, a branching onset is analyzed as containing two phonemes and not one. The branching onset shown in (4) contains two phonemes: a *p* followed by an *l*.

(4) O

We can retreat to a position whereby considerations of syllable structure do not enter into the defining properties of phonemes. In this case, we were wrong about the number of vowels in Latin; there are really only five. Each vowel can occur in branching or nonbranching nuclei, but that does not affect their phonemic status. Thus, length distinctions can be removed from considerations of phonemic status and assigned to syllable structure, where they belong.

Now what about tones? Consider a language with 4 tones and 10 vowels at the segmental level. Does this language have 10 vowels? 40 vowels (i.e., the 10 vowels times the 4 tones)? One would hesitate to say that a vowel with a high tone, say á, is completely different than the same vowel with a low tone, à. And yet by all the structuralist tests for contrast, these two segments meet the criteria for phonemehood. This question becomes all the more perplexing if we add some more factors. Let's start with a system of five vowels. Now we add four tones. Suppose this system has an ATR harmony. Now each vowel may occur as [+ATR] or [−ATR]. Finally, let's say that each vowel may have a nasal counterpart, a not uncommon property of West African languages.[3] How many vowels does this language have? A simple-minded answer would be:

(5) 5 vowels × 4 tones × 2 ATR values × 2 nasal values

This gives a whopping 80 vowel phonemes. But this seems intuitively wrong. One would like to say that this language has 5 vowels. Each vowel may carry any of the 4 tones, may occur as [+ATR] or [−ATR], and may be nasalized or not. If tones are taken to be external factors with respect to vowels, then why not ATR or nasality as well?

The question of nasality crops us again with respect to the Desano example discussed in the previous chapter. Voiced stops are realized in two ways in Desano: as voiced stops in an oral environment and as nasal consonants in a nasal environment. For example, the segment m is really a b plus an element of nasalization. In Desano, then, can we really say that m is a phoneme? The answer is far from obvious. But one might object that Desano is an exotic language. More familiar languages such as English do not raise the same difficulties with a segment as fundamental as m. Once more, appearances are misleading. English provides excellent evidence that m is a combination of a nasal consonant plus a labial stop. To see this, let's go back to our example of English nasal assimilation discussed in chapter 3.

(6) active   inactive   essential   inessential
     possible   impossible   balance   imbalance

---

tangible	intangible	tolerable	intolerable
complete	iŋcomplete/	credulous	iŋcredulous/
	incomplete		incredulous

Note the assimilation to a velar articulation is optional for some speakers. Recall that in the negative prefix *in-* the nasal consonant assimilates to the point or articulation of the following consonant. Thus *in-* plus *balance* gives *imbalance*. In SPE terms, this means that the nasal acquires the specifications of the features necessary to define the point of articulation (viz. [anterior], [coronal], [high], and [back]) from the following consonant. But once again we find that this process is arbitrary when expressed in a rule format. SPE does not assign a higher value to rules that copy feature specifications from contexts rather than, say, assigning one particular specification or even assigning the value opposite to that of the context. What is needed is an autosegmental representation where the process of nasal assimilation can be described in terms of spreading something from the context onto the target segment. In fact, if we look at the Desano facts, the solution to the English problem becomes much more obvious. In the case of the form *imbalance*, something has spread onto the nasal *n* to create an *m*. In Desano, a *b* in a nasal environment becomes *m*. We can combine both situations by proposing the formula,

(7) b + n = m

In the Desano case, it is the nasal element that spreads onto the various consonants and vowels. In English, it is the *b* that spreads onto the nasal, as shown in (8).

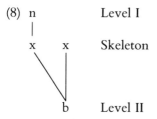

(8) n   Level I

     x   x   Skeleton

          b   Level II

In (8), the skeleton appears between two other levels, which I have called Level I and Level II. The nasal consonant occurs on Level I and the labial stop, on Level II. This latter segments spreads to the skeletal position to its left. We now have two units associated to a single point, *n* and *b*. According to the formula given in (7), this should yield an *m*.[4] This explains the *m* in

---

[4]The representation in (8) has, of course, been simplified in a number of respects. The

imbalance. Now, what do we think about *m?* Is it a phoneme? How does it differ from the Desano case, where nasal consonants seemed best analyzed as oral segments plus an element of nasality? The notion of phoneme seems to be getting fuzzier and fuzzier.

Let's return to another simple example: [wat] in French. How many phonemes are present in this form? In the case of *ouate,* this may depend on what syllabic analysis underlies a given speaker's behavior. Remember that [wat] has two possible syllabifications in French. These are given in (9).

(9) a.

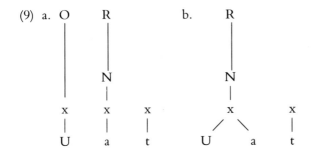

(9a) represents the case where *U* behaves like a consonant. This is the structure that underlies forms like *la ouate.* (9b) is the light diphthong case. This structure is present is forms like *l'ouate.* How many segments does this form have? Intuitively, it seems that (9a) has three segments. It behaves exactly like words such as *bec* [bek] 'kiss' or *sac* [sak] 'bag'. If *bec* and *sac* have three phonemes, the *ouate* of (9a) certainly does too. In (9b), the case is less clear. The sequence [wa] seems to behave as a unit. It occupies a single nuclear position. Is [wa] then a phoneme or a sequence of two phonemes? Calling the light diphthong a unit phoneme runs into more problems. Going back to the Dida example in chapter 4 we saw that light diphthongs could be created out of sequences of full-blown vowel segments. This happened every time we found a vowel sequence beginning with a high vowel and we deleted a skeletal point. We were left with two vowel segments attached to a single nucleus. In fact, diphthong formation in Dida exactly mirrors the formation of contour tones. One of the great contributions of early autosegmental theory was to show that contour tones are nothing but sequences of level tones.

By now, the moral should be abundantly clear: A phonology based on

---

details do not concern us here. What is important is the autosegmental behavior of the segment *b,* which is reflected in (8). The reader will have noted that *p* has the same effect on the preceding nasal as *b* (cf. *impossible*). A more complete analysis would show that this poses no particular problem. I used the case of *b* to bring out the parallelism with the Desano example.

nonlinear, multileveled representations is incompatible with the notion of a phoneme. There is no longer any place to look for such an entity. Autosegmental levels have invaded every aspect of phonological structure. What I have called the segmental level earlier in this book was nothing more than a convenient fiction. We have broken this level open in many of our examples only to reveal the existence of further levels. No one level seems to stand out among the others. The center of phonological structure, if it exists at all, is certainly the skeleton, a sequence of timing units stripped of any phonetic content.[5] Phonological segments are exactly what the theory says they are: associations of a variety of units on a variety of levels linked to one or more points of the skeleton. Where the phoneme fits into all this is far from obvious. It now seems pointless to even look for it. The lesson of modern phonological theory is clear: The phoneme is dead.

SOME IMPLICATIONS OF CURRENT RESEARCH

Phonologists (and perhaps linguists in general) are always hard pressed to respond to the question, so what? It is all very nice to know that phonological systems are not a random collection of arbitrary phenomena but are rather highly structured and quite restricted in scope. But what earthly good is it to know that phonological representations consist of a series of discrete levels with a skeletal core all connected in a latticework of association lines? One can always take refuge in the "science is its own reward" or "any advancement in our knowledge ennobles humanity" type of response. I happen to be one of those who believe in these kinds of answers. On the other hand, it is satisfying to see the results of research applied to something more concrete. Happily, the recent developments of phonological theory coincide with rapid growth of the computer industry.

One of the earliest attempts to combine certain aspects of linguistics and computers came in the 1950s. From the earliest period of computers, the idea of machine translation (MT) was a natural. Filled with confidence, researchers believed that it was only a question of time before a workable and economic system could be developed for translating written text from one language to the other. The economic advantages of such a system were and are such that a good number of private corporations were ready to invest significant sums of money in the hope of developing such a system. Imagine typing a text onto your computer screen, pressing a function key,

---

[5]There is a version of nonlinear phonology that proposes a CV tier (C for consonant, V for vowel) rather than a skeleton. In this version, the skeleton does contain some minimal phonetic information concerning the syllabicity of the associated segments. However, the essential point remains even in this version.

and having the translation come up in the language of your choice. Consider the problem of such multilingual institutions as the UN, the EEC, and the Government of Canada with respect to translating tens of thousands of pages into different languages. It does not take long to convince oneself of the utility and the profitability of a working MT system. In fact, the efforts to develop such a system ended in dismal defeat. MT projects have been in near total abeyance for the past decade.[6] It is instructive to try and understand the reasons for the failure of MT projects. Doing so may help us to avoid in future endeavors the kinds of fundamental mistakes that I believe characterized these projects.

There is an understandable friction that almost inevitably develops between theoretical linguists and engineers working on projects such as MT. The linguist is naturally interested in problems involving the nature of human language, its universal properties, how it is organized, and so on. The engineer has a job to do: get the system up and working. Theoretical questions of linguistics are largely irrelevant to the task at hand. Who cares how human beings operate? What we need is a cost-effective program that will get the job done. There is a general belief that the results of linguistic theory are of no real use for practical projects of this kind. It is not surprising then that MT research took place in the virtual absence of any results of syntactic theory, at least in its beginnings. In all fairness, there was an excellent reason for this, independent of anyone's feelings toward linguistics: There was virtually no syntactic theory available before 1957.[7] Truly applicable versions of the theory became available around 1970 with the advent of what has been called the extended standard theory. An enormous amount of progress has been made in our understanding of the nature of syntactic structure. But old habits die hard, and even current MT projects are not marked by the utilization of the latest results of syntactic theory. It is not surprising then that these atheoretic approaches have not met with great success. It would be hard to imagine the great technological achievements of this century being based on methods that systematically ignored the results of theoretical physics.

Taking an example closer to home—that is, closer to phonology—consider the case of automatic speech recognition (ASR). The idea of ASR is to develop a system whereby the user speaks into a microphone hooked up to the computer and either the computer acts directly on the command or else puts it up on the screen. Once again, the interest and the practicality of such a system are obvious. In fact, primitive versions of such a system, capable of

---

[6]There are some recent attempts to take another crack at the MT project. From what I have learned of such projects, they appear to stand no better chance at success than their predecessors.

[7]This is the year in which Noam Chomsky's *Syntactic structures* appeared (Chomsky, 1957).

recognizing several hundred commands under certain circumstances, have been developed. The ultimate goal, of course, is to construct an open system: one that is not limited to a certain repertory of items but rather can recognize any well-formed expression in a given language. Obviously, questions of spelling need to be handled by such a system because what is usually desired is a correct written version of what is said into the microphone. These problems are quite minor and can be handled by existing software. The real problem is getting something onto the screen, never mind how it's spelled.

In general, current research in ASR seems to be following the same procedure as that of MT. Much time is being spent developing systems capable of recognizing phonemes. If the results of phonological theory are correct, this is a vain search. There are no phonemes. This is a rather trivial example as well as a negative one. It is all very well to criticize ongoing research, but does phonological theory have anything better to offer? I think it does. It is quite clear that phonological representations take the form of a series of interconnected layers. Each layer or tier has a small set of elements proper to it. These tiers behave in more or less the same manner. What this means in simple terms is that the number of possibilities of the form of phonological representations is quite limited. Second, the divergence between the ultimate output of a phonological derivation and its underlying source is extremely restricted. This seems to be an enormous clue as to how the ASR problem might be solved. The one fully operational ASR system available to us, the system used by human beings, certainly takes full advantage of these restrictions. People and machines generally do much better at detecting a given item when the item goes from a very small set rather than from an unbounded set. Imagine a number being flashed on the screen for one-sixteenth of a second. Our chances of identifying the number are obviously improved if we are told that it comes from a set that includes only 13 and 23,476. This may seem a bit extreme, but the point remains true. The spoken chain is not some random assortment of frequencies, varying in indefinitely many ways. It represents a highly structured sequence of events. If we know what the structure is, this will go a long way toward solving the ASR problem. We are now starting to have a pretty good idea of just what phonological representations can and do look like.

THE ROBUSTNESS OF THE SPEECH SIGNAL

There is another fundamental fact about our communicative system that, it seems to me, must be taken into account in order for progress in problems such as ASR to take place. Our communicative system is incredibly robust. To best understand and appreciate how robust human language is, it is worth considering systems that do not share this property. Programming languages are notorious examples of this. They are most fragile. If I am writing a BASIC program and I enter the statement:

(10) 25 PRIMT "Hello world!"

upon executing the program containing statement 25, I will get BASIC's terse comment, "Syntax error." Eventually (depending on how late at night it is), I will notice that I have misspelled the command *PRINT* as *PRIMT*. A human reacting to this situation would exclaim, "You idiot! How can you not know that I meant 'PRINT' when I wrote 'PRIMT'! What else could it be!" This is fragility. The slightest deviation from the expected results in total incomprehension.

Human language is not like this at all. It can withstand all kinds of distortions, noise, chopping out of its upper frequency range (as in telephones), and general abuse. The message gets through. I can talk with peanuts in my mouth or after four drinks of Scotch or with a bad head cold and still the message gets through. We can generally understand an impressive variety of foreign accents, young children, and even synthesized speech. We can understand this in a background that can include jackhammers or the Rolling Stones. This is robust! There is an interesting experiment that anyone who speaks a second language reasonably well, but not perfectly, can perform. Engage someone who speaks your second language in conversation. Presumably, you have no difficulty in understanding. Now, either turn up the radio or walk into another room while your interlocutor continues speaking. You will notice that your comprehension level drops dramatically. Try doing the same thing while someone is speaking your native language. The difference should be quite striking. Even the small degree of linguistic competence that distinguishes a native speaker from a fluent second language speaker can have perceptible effects on robustness. Phonological representations are strictly organized, but we have to know, that is, have internal knowledge of, what the organization is. The parametric differences that define distinct languages are sufficient to bring comprehension to a screeching halt. Indeed, the general impression of hearing a foreign language for the first time is one of noise. Individual words are not perceived. As one internalizes the phonological and syntactic systems that underlie this language, the veil slowly lifts and discernible patterns— words, phrases, sentences—begin to emerge. This is how our own ASR system works.

How can our system be so robust? The key word here is redundancy.[8]

---

[8]In fact, this is a misnomer. The traditional definition of redundancy is unnecessary repetition. Indeed, often it isn't really repetition but multiple sources of information. Here, the repetition is anything but unnecessary.

The speech signal must be bristling with cues for various aspects of phonological structure. The loss of one or even several of these cues does not unduly lower the efficacy of our internal ASR system. Some small indication of the degree of redundancy is found in studying the results of data compression. There are a number of algorithms for reducing the size (measured in bytes) of data files. Compression algorithms are useful when transmission time or storage space is a factor. Uploading or downloading from a BBS (an electronic bulletin board) typically involves compressed files. The amount of space saved by compression techniques varies according to the type of file. Text files (i.e., files in normal written English or some other natural language) may be reduced by as much as 70%. In contrast, binary files (files containing executable code) are typically reduced by only 5% to 10%. It is true that written English is only a pale imitation of the spoken language. The degree of compressibility with no information lost does give us some indication as to the level of redundancy of the spoken chain. We can safely assume that cues are plastered across the speech signal in very broad strokes. In sum, they should be very hard to miss. Distorting the signal in various ways may modify or destroy some of these cues. Enough remain for intelligibility to be maintained. Knowledge of what these cues are and how they are organized within phonological structure can provide important clues for the construction of ASR systems. It is precisely this kind of information that phonological theory provides.

Consider the case of syllable structure. This level of representation imposes severe constraints on what segments can occur in a given position. Syllable structure may be thought of as first-order organization of the speech signal. That is, without worrying about the identity of actual segments, it should be possible to deduce the number of syllables from the raw signal. I am *not* suggesting that syllable structure can be read directly off the speech signal. Syllable theory will dictate what kinds of (abstract) structures may be posited, given the input signal. I am talking about a cognitive system serving to interpret in fixed and predetermined ways the speech signal. This kind of scenario is similar to the kinds of strategies developed in vision research. Our cognitive system fills in the raw input, consisting of a series of intensity readings, allowing the construction of the final image. Seeing an edge involves applying a (tacit) theory of edges to the raw signal. Hearing syllable structure involves applying syllable theory to the raw signal. Just as the brain can be fooled into seeing edges where none exist, we can hear syllable constituents that are not present in the input signal. Syllable theory enhances the input signal and allows for interpretation in a variety of conditions. A reasonable first step in the construction of an ASR system would be a syllable recognizer: a device that assigns syllable structure to the input signal. Let's consider how such a device could work and how it could be employed in a bootstrapping operation to eventually arrive at a phonological representation of the speech signal. For obvious reasons, I only give a bare bones sketch of this hypothetical device, skipping over a number of important and difficult questions. The point I wish to make is that knowledge of phonological theory (in this case syllable theory) can offer interesting and *practical* solutions to the ASR problem.

Syllable structure can be thought of as a series of onset–rime sequences. Internal to these sequences is a fundamental opposition of noise and resonance. The former characterizes onsets and the latter, rimes. At this stage, we are seeking the segmental identity of the onset or the rime. We are simply noting their presence in the signal. Let's pretend that the acoustic cues that distinguish onset from rimes are gross enough that a detector could be constructed to pick them out of the speech signal. This detector needn't be 100% accurate. It should be able to deal with the nonproblematic cases. I assume that the input *pa* would be one of the nonproblematic cases. With this input, the device might give the following output:

(11) *Input:* pa   *Output* O   R
                          pa

If onsets always accompany rimes, then even hearing one sonority peak would be sufficient to assign the output structure. The remaining problem is to identify the segmental content of the onset and of the rime. We now have a substantial advantage over a system that does not employ syllable structure: Syllable theory tells us what the possible onsets and what the possible rimes are. To the extent that we can narrow down the possibilities, the ultimate detection of the phonological representation becomes easier. The task still appears formidable. A language may have as many as 40 segments capable of occurring in the onset position. A smaller but still impressive number of different segments may occur in the rime. What is important here is that, as a first step, assigning syllable structure to a string will cut down on the number of possibilities involving its ultimate constituents. Closer examination of the theory of syllable structure and the choice of more complex examples would show that in many cases the choices for a given position are considerably more restricted.

Be that as it may, the idea of choosing from among up to 40 candidate segments for an onset position is quite misleading. We are going back to our old habits of thinking in terms of unit phonemes. But phonological theory shows that this is not how things are organized. Phonological segments are not units but rather combinations of elements present on the various levels of representation. To this point, I have not discussed the exact nature of these elements. Are they features or something else? I take up this question in the following section.

THE ULTIMATE PHONOLOGICAL UNITS

We have followed the progression of phonological theory from atomic phonemes to feature matrices to interconnected autosegmental units in a multilinear representation. It is reasonable to ask what type of animal an autosegment is. To the extent that phonologists have expressed an opinion on the subject, it has often been assumed that autosegments are simply features detached from the segmental matrix and assigned to another level of structure. There is another point of view, one which I share, that rejects the feature as the ultimate phonological unit. In this latter view, segments are composed of pronounceable feature packets, called *elements*.[9] To get a handle on this type of representation, it is easiest to use a chemical metaphor. Segments are either elements or combinations of elements. The element itself is at least potentially pronounceable in its pristine form. Elements may combine to form the phonological equivalent of compounds: segments consisting of more than one element. I spare the reader the technical details of this theory and give a simple example of how this theory may be applied to vowel systems. This example has the advantage of receiving similar treatment by the three nonfeature approaches listed earlier.

Suppose we posit three elements that underlie vowel systems. I represent these elements with the capital letters A, I, and U. They are quite pronounceable in isolation, that is, in their pure form.

(12) *Element*   *Pronunciation*
    A   as in father
    I   as in see
    U   as in boot

Each element may be thought of as a complete feature matrix that specifies all the details of its pronunciation. The phonology does not have access to these features. The only items that are manipulated are the elements. The definitions of the elements are simply score cards to assure ourselves that we are indeed representing what we want to represent.

The Arabic language has a system of three vowels. Interestingly, these vowels correspond exactly to the elements listed in (12).

(13) *The Arabic Vowels*
      i   u
         a

---

[9]There are three different schools that follow a nonfeature approach to phonological representations. These schools differ from one another in some important ways, but they share the basic insight that I discuss here. *Dependency phonology* (Anderson & Jones, 1974) enjoys histor-

This is all very well for Arabic. There, we have a case where each vowel of the system corresponds to one of our elements. We know, however, that other vowels exist. How can they be represented based on our system of three elements? As the chemical metaphor suggests, vowels may consist of combinations of elements. Take the case of Latin. It has five vowels:

(14) *The Latin Vowels*

    i   u

    e   o

          a

The vowels *i, u,* and *a* correspond to each of the elements in its pure form. The remaining vowels, *e* and *o,* are compounds. In (15) I give an informal model of the Latin system.

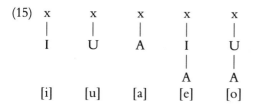

(15)

The representation of the first three vowels is clear. They are the elements in isolation. The final two vowels are compounds. I represent them by linking the two elements together with an association line, and the combined expression is in turn linked to a skeletal point. We see that *e* is a combination of A and I; *o* is a combination of A and U.

Languages, through changes or processes, often give us clear indications of the internal structure of segments. We can often witness cases of disintegration (the pulling apart) of segments. A compound segment can decompose into a sequence of its constituent parts. One example of such decomposition comes from the Kugpeela dialect of Mooré, a Gur language spoken in the West African country of Burkina Faso (Nikiema, 1986).

(16) *Singluar*   *Plural*   *Translation*
      pòò-ré   pwàyá   back

What is of interest here is the behavior of the stem vowel. In the singular form, it appears as a long vowel, *oo.* In the plural form, we note the loss of a

---

ical precedence. *Particle phonology* (Schane, 1984) is the second school. I have had a hand in the creation of *charm and government theory* (Kaye, Lowenstamm, & Vergnaud, 1985, in press), the third of these schools, and so my discussion is based on this latter theory.

skeletal point and the decomposition of the compound vowel *o*. These changes are motivated by some arcane reasons that do not concern us here. In our new notation the process looks like (17).

(17)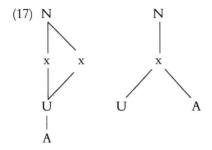

The singular form has a compound vowel association to both nuclear points, yielding a long *oo*. In the plural form, we have lost a skeletal point, and the compound vowel has decomposed into its constituents, *U* and *A*. Both elements associate to the only available point, giving us a light diphthong [wa]. Nothing need be said about the order in which these elements occur. A light diphthong requires that a high vowel precede the remaining vowel.

The opposite effect can be observed in the historical development of (standard) French. A compound vowel was formed over the course of time from a sequence of its constituents. Many French words spelled with *ai* and *au* used to be pronounced as heavy diphthongs. The words *fait* 'fact' and *paume* 'palm of the hand' illustrate this change. Today, these words contain the vowels *e* and *o*, respectively. What used to be the heavy diphthong [ay] is now [e], what used to be the heavy diphthong [aw] is now [o]. The formal aspects of this change are shown in (18).

(18)

The internal structure of our compound vowels is revealed clearly by this change. *A* and *I* have combined to form an *e*; *A* and *U* have combined to form an *o*. Examples of both types could easily be multiplied.

A certain number of phonological processes can now be expressed in terms of composition and decomposition. The relevant units are the elements. Of course, to express the full richness of the segmental possibilities we need more than the three elements just presented. What is interesting is that their number is not very large and that the same elements can be found in the internal structure of both consonants and vowels. Manipulating elements in this way constitutes a further cutback in the expressive power of phonological theory. Gone are the days when we could play fast and loose with various features and their specifications. Now, all we can do is put elements together to form compound segments and pull them apart, as in cases of decomposition. This does not allow for a large number of possibilities given an initial structure. To the extent that this more restricted theory provides a good fit with the observed phenomena, we can maintain a certain confidence that we are on the right track. At present, we can point to an impressive area of phonological phenomena that are simply and adequately accounted for in this formalism.

There are also interesting implications for our earlier discussion regarding ASR systems. Simply put, elements make conveniently large targets for a device whose job it is to detect them. Trying to detect individual features in a speech signal has proved rather difficult. A single, phonologically defined feature may appear in a variety of disguises according to the context in which it occurs. The problem of looking for a cue or several cues that signal its presence in the signal is accordingly more difficult. A feature specification such as [+high] may have no single immutable phonetic interpretation. Its identification would depend on the presence of other feature specifications, which, in turn, may prove equally ethereal. An element, being a feature packet, may get around this problem.

The nature of phonological representations offers further aid for the detection of elements. Quite frequently, elements are plastered over more than one skeletal position. An element found as part of a compound segment may occur in isolation in a neighboring position. This gives us two chances at identifying it. Palatalization provides us with such a case. We have seen that frequently a coronal stop or fricative is palatalized before the vowel *i*. Thus, an underlying sequence *ti* is realized as *či* in a large number of languages. In our new system of notation, palatalization is nothing more than the spreading of the element *I* onto the preceding coronal consonant.

(19)

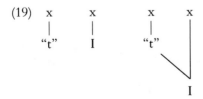

It should be noted that "*t*" is simply an abbreviation for the combination of elements that constitute this segment. The point is, whatever the internal structure of "*t*" may be, *č* can be represented as the combination of "*t*" and the element *I*. We see in (19) that this element manifests itself twice: once in combination with "*t*" to produce *č*, and once in isolation to produce the vowel [i].

It is equally interesting to note that the segmental makeup of a form undergoing palatalization does not change. Suppose that the morphemes of a language are accessed according to their segmental composition. A phonological change such as that in (19) is then completely transparent to this accessing system. We are looking for a form that has a "*t*" and an *I*. The process of palatalization does not change this. "*t*" and *I* are still present in the output form; they are just arranged somewhat differently. This kind of representational invariance can simplify any matching routine whose job is to relate a lexical form with part of the speech signal. Representing phonological processes as in (19) offers three advantages for a system of signal decoding: (a) the target units to be identified may be present at several positions, (b) the segmental composition of the string in terms of elements does not change, and (c) the process itself indicates that there is no major constituent boundary between the two points to which the element is linked. If we know in advance that phonological processes have this formal property, that is, if we believe the results of phonological research, strategies for ASR construction can be modified to take advantage of this additional knowledge.

Obviously, I have only given the briefest glimpse of an element-based theory of phonological representations. The theory contains principles dictating which elements can readily combine with which others, what the limits of parametric variation are among phonological systems, what sequences of segments can occur within a phonological domain, what restrictions there are on the occurrence of segments in given syllabic positions, and so on. The good news is that we are in the process of reducing what appears to be a bewildering variety of phonological phenomena to a few elementary formal operations. The picture that emerges is unmistakable: Phonological representations are highly organized structures that obey very tight restrictions. Knowledge of the structure of phonological representations and their limits can provide important clues to the way ASR systems, learning systems, and parsers can be constructed. The thrust of my argument is that phonology has the form it does precisely because of our own human needs in these areas.

My purpose in writing this book has been to acquaint the reader with a range of problems surrounding the study of sound systems as they are found in human languages. I have tried to give a broad idea of what phonologists do and why I believe it is worth doing. In making the research problems of phonology accessible to the nonlinguist and in keeping this book to a reasonable length, I have skipped over many interesting and important areas of phonology. Many of the theories and the analyses based on them could be presented in much greater detail. I have not noted the myriad of problems that surround any attempt to say something new and interesting. Clearly, theoretical advances always involve saying something nonobvious and often apparently false. At every stage, legitimate questions can be posed. I do not wish to give the impression that there is general agreement on all the points I have discussed in this book. Scrutinizing each theoretical point will reveal a variety of positions that surround it. Nevertheless, I feel the overall picture is fairly accurate. Phonology has progressed in the last 20 years. There is a general, if not universal, shift toward nonlinear systems. Rule-based approaches are being replaced by more restricted theories in a widening area of phonological structure. I certainly do not believe that the last word has been said regarding any of the issues I have raised. To make progress in a field is not reason for complacency but rather for more intense efforts. Each problem generates a family of solutions. Theoretical diversity is a healthy sign and can only benefit the field as a whole. As sure as I am that much remains to be done, that many of our current assumptions will fall by the wayside, I also know that the phonology of today is more interesting, more exciting, and more fun to do than it was 20 years ago. As Noam Chomsky has often said in assessing progress in linguistics, perhaps now we are beginning to make interesting mistakes.

References

Anderson, J., & Jones, C. (1974). Three theses concerning phonological representations. *Journal of Linguistics, 10,* 1–26.

Chomsky, N. (1957). *Syntactic structures.* The Hague: Mouton.

Chomsky, N., & Halle, M. (1968). *The sound pattern of English.* New York: Harper & Row.

Dresher, E., & Kaye, J. D. (in press). A computer-based learning theory for metrical phonology. *Cognition.*

Firth, J. R. (1948). Sounds and prosodies. *Transaction of the Philological Society, 46,* 127–152.

Goldsmith, J. (1976). *Autosegmental phonology.* Unpublished doctoral dissertation, Massachusetts Institute of Technology.

Hagège, C. (1976). *La grammaire générative: réflexions critiques* [Generative grammar: Some critical reflections]. Vendôme: Presses Universitaires de France.

Halle, M., & Vergnaud, J.-R. (1987). *An essay on stress.* Cambridge, MA: MIT Press.

Harris, Z. (1944). Simultaneous components in phonology. *Language, 20,* 181–205.

Hayes, B. (1980). *A metrical theory of stress rules.* Unpublished doctoral dissertation, Massachusetts Institute of Technology.

Joos, M. (1958). *Readings in linguistics.* New York: American Council of Learned Societies.

Kahn, D. (1976). *Syllable-based generalizations in English phonology.* Unpublished doctoral dissertation, Massachusetts Institute of Technology.

Kaye, J. D., & Charette, M. (1981). Tone sensitive rules in Dida. *Studies in African Linguistics, 12*(Suppl. 8), 82–85.

Kaye, J. D., & Lowenstamm, J. (1984). De la Syllabicite (On syllabicity). In F. Dell, D. Hirst, & J.-R. Vergnaud (Eds.), *Forme sonore du langage.* Paris: Hermann.

Kaye, J. D., Lowenstamm, J., & Vergnaud, J.-R. (1985). The internal structure of phonological elements: A theory of charm and government. *Phonology Yearbook, 2,* 305–328.

Kaye, J. D., Lownstamm, J., & Vergnaud, J.-R. (in press). Constituent structure & government in phonology. In M. Prinzhorn (Ed.), *Linguistiche Berichte.*

Kaye, J. D., & Roosen-Runge, P. (1973). *A user's guide to the phonological calculator.* Toronto: University of Toronto.

167

Lass, R. (1984). *Phonology: An introduction to basic concepts*. Cambridge, England: Cambridge University Press.

Leben, W. (1973). *Suprasegmental phonology*. Unpublished doctoral dissertation, Massachusetts Institute of Technology.

Liberman, M., & Prince, A. (1977). On stress and linguistic rhythm. *Linguistic Inquiry, 8*, 249–336.

Lovins, J. (1971). Melodic conspiracies in Lomongo tonology. *Papers from the Seventh Regional Meeting of the Chicago Linguistics Society, 0*, 469–478.

McCarthy, J. (1979). *Formal problems in Semitic phonology and morphology*. Unpublished doctoral dissertation, Massachusetts Institute of Technology.

Morgan, J. (in preparation). *Linguistics: Its implications for cognitive science*. Hillsdale, NJ: Lawrence Erlbaum Associates.

Nikiema, E. (1986). *Niveau syllabique et structures radicales en mooré* [The syllable level and root structures in Mooré]. Unpublished master's essay, University of Quebec, Montreal.

Phillips, C. (1971). *A phonological parser*. Unpublished master's essay, University of Toronto, Toronto.

Pulleyblank, D. (1983). *Tone in lexical phonology*. Unpublished doctoral dissertation, Massachusetts Institute of Technology.

Schane, S. (1984). The fundamentals of particle phonology. *Phonology Yearbook, 1*, 32–51.

Trubetzkoy, N. (1958). *Grundzüge der Phonologie* [Principles of phonology]. Göttingen: Vandenhoeck & Ruprecht.

Waterson, N. (1956). Some aspects of the phonology of the nominal forms of the Turkish word. *Bulletin of the School of Oriental and African Studies, 18*, 578–591.

Weinreich, U. (1958). A retrograde sound shift in the guise of a survival. *Miscelánea Homenaje a André Martinet. Vol. 2* (pp. 221–267). Canary Isles: Biblioteca Filológica. Universidad de la Laguna.

Whorf, B. (1956). *Language, thought, and reality*. Cambridge, MA: MIT Press.

Williams, E. (1976). Underlying tone in Margi and Igbo. *Linguistic Inquiry, 7*, 463–484.

Author Index

Subject Index